W9-BUG-278

The
CONTEMPORARY
DICTIONARY

of
SEXUAL
EUPHEMISMS

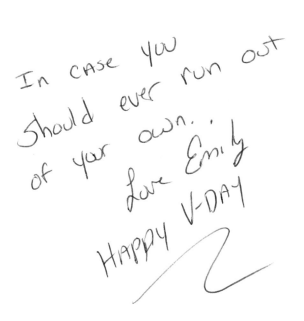

In case you
Should ever run out
of your own...
Love Emily
HAPPY V-DAY

The
CONTEMPORARY
DICTIONARY
of
SEXUAL
EUPHEMISMS

Jordan Tate

ST. MARTIN'S PRESS

New York

THE CONTEMPORARY DICTIONARY OF SEXUAL EUPHEMISMS. Copyright © 2007 by Jordan Tate. All rights reserved. Printed in the United States of America. No part of this book may be used or reproduced in any manner whatsoever without written permission except in the case of brief quotations embodied in critical articles or reviews. For information, address St. Martin's Press, 175 Fifth Avenue, New York, N.Y. 10010.

www.stmartins.com

All photographs by the author

Book design by Jonathan Bennett

Library of Congress Cataloging-in-Publication Data

Tate, Jordan.
    The contemporary dictionary of sexual euphemisms / Jordan
Tate.—1st U.S. ed.
        p. cm.
    ISBN-13: 978-0-312-36298-0
    ISBN-10: 0-312-36298-6
        1. Sex—Dictionaries. 2. English language—Jargon—Dictionaries.
    I. Title.
HQ9.36 2007
306.703—dc22

                                                        2006051162

First Edition: January 2007

10 9 8 7 6 5 4 3 2 1

ACKNOWLEDGMENTS

Many thanks to the following people for being photo models:
David Hanus, James Tate, Matt Griffin, Courtney Terell, Drew Renslow, Galo Moncayo, Karen Green, Sarah Ellsworth, Sam York, Alyson Gross, Marie Woods, Ethan Ransdell, Arthur Hash, Kelly O'Malley, James Francis Flynn, Brandi Bunfill, Brent McGill, Genevieve Johnson, Adriana Keaton, Paris Brewer, Noah Everitt, Liz Wepeler, and Jordan Wood.

INTRODUCTION

The sexual euphemism originated from society's inability to accept sexuality as a normal part of existence. It was a mark of shame to have desire. The euphemism has been used as a shield against these judgments and has more recently been adopted by contemporary masculinity to be used as both shield and weapon. Contemporary masculinity is a fragile thing that is easily threatened by any form of change or emasculation. It is because of this that the lexicon of sexual euphemisms has several distinct categories. If examined, it is easy to decipher how and why these euphemisms were created to empower masculinity which, since the women's movement, has become increasingly unstable and threatened. It is masculinity that stands as a threat to itself, and the euphemism is merely salting the wound. The inability of masculinity to define itself independent of femininity, rather than proclaiming itself as the antithesis of femininity, is catapulted to the forefront of society by the form and structure of the sexual euphemisms presented in these pages.

E. J. COLLINS, PH.D., UNIVERSITY OF WASHINGTON, 1976

The
CONTEMPORARY
DICTIONARY

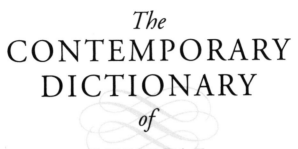

of
SEXUAL
EUPHEMISMS

AC/DC, adj.

1. An indication that a device is capable of operation with a power supply of either alternating or direct current.
2. AC/DC was a pioneering rock band founded in 1973 by brothers Angus and Malcolm Young and is considered one of the most influential bands of this century.
3. Bisexual. (slang)

AC, abbreviation for alternating current c.1800, Middle English; and DC, abbreviation for direct current, c.1650, Middle English.

EX. Jimmy bought a new adapter for his portable television; he was happy because it was *AC/DC.*

AC/DC is a term used to describe the tendency of any person to engage in sexual congress with members of either gender. The use of this term is rooted in the two primary forms of electricity and the ability of some devices to use either type. Ironically, AC is enough to indicate an oscillation of sexual tendency, but the addition of DC (direct current) is used as a further signifier to reinforce the sexual preference.

back·door bur·glar, n.

1. A thief who intends to commit or commits burglary of a movable structure used to close off an entrance, typically consisting of a panel that swings on hinges or that slides or rotates in the rear entrance of a domicile or business.
2. One who commits larceny by means of approach or access to the rear of the building.
3. Any person engaging in anal congress. (slang)
4. Homosexual. (slang) (specifically male) (often considered offensive)

Middle English *bak,* from Old English *bæc;* Middle English *dor,* from Old English *duru, dor.* See *dhwer-* in Indo-European roots; and Anglo-Norman *burgler* (alteration of *burgesur,* probably from Old French *burg, borough*), Medieval Latin *burgultor* (alteration of *burgtor,* from *burgre,* to commit burglary in, from Late Latin *burgus,* fortified town) both of Germanic origin. See *bhergh* in Indo-European Roots.

EX. Many of the citizens of the city of Dallas were missing their screen doors due to a rash of larceny suspected to originate from a gang of *backdoor burglars.*

Backdoor burglar, much like *turd burglar* and *backdoor butler,* is a reference to a homosexual man. The act of burglary implies loose morals and a person shunned from proper society. This term was born out of midwestern American homophobia in the early twentieth century. It was the understanding of these people that any person who would commit sodomy had a propensity for other so-called immoral activities, such as larceny. This euphemism has very negative and judgmental connotations on the behavioral choices of homosexual men. Although this euphemism can also be applied to any person who engages in anal intercourse, it is generally reserved for homosexual men as an insult to their person and character.

Backdoor burglar, n.

back·door but·ler, n.

1. The male head servant in a large or important household, with responsibilities that include overseeing the other staff, taking care of the wine and silverware, and sometimes receiving guests in secrecy or in a surreptitious way, often through the rear entrance of the household.
2. Homosexual. (slang)(specifically male) (often considered offensive)
3. Any purveyor of anal congress. (slang)

From Middle English *bak,* from Old English *bæc; dor,* from Old English *duru, dor.* See *dhwer-* in Indo-European Roots; and Middle English, from Old French *bouteillier,* bottle bearer, from *bouteille, botele,* bottle.

EX. When Alice and Gerald went to leave their domicile, they were pleased to find the *backdoor butler* on duty.

The origins of *backdoor butler* are rooted in the individual definitions of the words. Here backdoor is a reference to the anus, and butler (derived from the French use of the term) is a reference to someone who graciously ushers a guest into the home (or backdoor) and tends to any needs the guest may have. So, this term is used to describe what is known as the "bottom," the male in a homosexual interaction who ushers his partner into his anus and tends to his needs while "inside."

Backdoor butler, n.

beat your meat, v.

1. To hit or strike repeatedly the edible flesh of animals, especially that of mammals as opposed to that of fish or poultry.
2. To subject the edible part, as of a piece of fruit, a nut, or a mammal, to repeated beatings or physical abuse.
3. Male masturbation. (slang)

Middle English *beten,* from Old English *baten,* See *bhau-* in Indo-European Roots; and Middle English *mete,* from Old English, *food.*

EX. Because Ryan was having company over for dinner and wanted to make a good impression, he *beat the meat* thoroughly so his guests could enjoy its tenderness.

Beat your meat was one of the first recorded sexual euphemisms due to its simplicity and its reference to an act that is not obscure or foreign. People would regularly have to tenderize meat prior to consumption by repeated blows to the fleshy part of the cured meats. This was first used as a euphemism in the British Isles. Referring to the penis as the "meat" is merely a reference to many fine cuts of meat and the shape of the penis, due to the simplicity of this reference, it has now come to be used in the common vernacular. These cuts were generally expensive and saved for special occasions often included the filet (beef) and the tenderloins (pork, lamb), with the use of loins another obvious parallel. Men spread this euphemism in order to instill a sense of preciousness to the cultural perception of their penises.

beef cur·tains, n.

1. The flesh of a slaughtered full-grown steer that hangs in a window or other opening as a decoration, shade, or screen.
2. A full-grown steer, bull, ox, or cow, especially one intended for use as meat that functions as or resembles a screen, cover, or barrier.
3. Labia. (slang)

Middle English, from Old French *buef,* from Latin *bs, bov-.* See *gwou-* in Indo-European roots; and the Middle English *cortine,* from Old French, from Late Latin *crtna,* from Latin *crs, crt-,* variant of *cohors, court.*

EX. Adriana was making a haunted dollhouse for Halloween, so she bought some roast beef to make *beef curtains.*

The use of *beef curtains* as a sexual euphemism derives from the study of anatomy. The function of a curtain, much like the function of the outer labia, is to cover an opening or orifice (a window or vulva). Originating in midwestern America in the early twentieth century, it was merely a reference used in breeding steer with female cattle. The insemination process involved manually stimulating the bull to the point of ejaculation and inserting the semen into the vagina of the female cow (after first having to spread the labia in order to insert the semen). This act inspired the use of the term *beef curtains* in a wider context. Without much delay, this term crept off of the farm and into the lexicon of sexual euphemisms.

Bev·er·ly hill·bil·ly, n.

1. A person from the backwoods or the remote mountain area surrounding a city of northeast Massachusetts (Beverly) northeast of Boston. It was settled in 1626. The schooner *Hannah,* the first ship of the Continental Navy, was outfitted here (1775). Population: 39,862 at 2000 census.

2. A character from the popular sitcom created by Paul Henning (of *Petticoat Junction* fame), which ran on CBS from 1963–70. The premise of the show (which is detailed by the theme song) surrounds the sudden onset of wealth by poor aim rather than hard work and his family.

3. A sexual act whereby—while attempting to perform cunnilingus—the performing participant performs analingus (whether intentional or not).

Middle English, from Old English *fre.* See *aiw-* in Indo-European roots; and Middle English *hil,* from Old English *hyll.* See *kel-2* in Indo-European roots, and *Hill-Billie* first recorded in the April 23, 1900, *New York Journal:* "In short, a Hill-Billie is a free and untrammelled white citizen of Alabama, who lives in the hills, has no means to speak of, dresses as he can, talks as he pleases, drinks whiskey when he gets it, and fires off his revolver as the fancy takes him."

EX. Every day after school, Adam would dress up like Jed Clampett and pretend he was a *Beverly hillbilly.*

The *Beverly hillbilly* is one of the forerunners of the categories of euphemisms that contain inherent prejudice to the American south. Also in this category are the "southern trespass" (also known as the "General Lee") and the "Kentucky stirfry." The origin of these terms all involve anal intercourse or analingus of some sort as a reference to backwards southern sexual practices (additionally referencing the position of the anus in relation to the vagina during a large percentage of sexual activity) and the general perceived intelligence level of its residents. Although postdating the General Lee and the Kentucky stirfry by almost a century, the Beverly hillbilly spread like wildfire through American culture after the show's popularity in 1962. The derisive aspect of the euphemism arises from the southern citizens' assumed ineptitude and stupidity in mistaking the vagina for the anus. Furthermore, the discovery of "black gold" is seen as a fortuitous event, thereby affirming that southerners enjoy performing analingus and also maintain a lack of hygiene to the point that there is excrement outside of the sphincter.

black tie af·fair, n.

1. Semiformal evening wear typically for men, usually requiring a dinner jacket and worn for something done or to be done generally for business.
2. Transactions and other matters of professional or public business that require a bow tie and dinner jacket.
3. A sexual act that involves adorning a prostitute in fine attire in order to engage in sexual activity.

Middle English *blak,* from Old English *blæc.* See *bhel-*1 in Indo-European roots; Middle English *tien,* from Old English *tgan.* See *deuk-* in Indo-European roots; and Middle English *affaire,* from Old French *afaire,* from *à faire,* to do: *a, to* from Latin ad. See *ad-+faire,* to do from *facere.* See *dh-* in Indo-European roots.

EX. Richard dressed up Julia and they went to a *black tie affair.*

The *black tie affair* (also known as the "pretty woman") is not necessarily a sexual act, but the actions leading up to, which sets it apart in the lexicon of sexual euphemisms. It is not infrequent that any man, being of high social status or not, will feel the need for coitus and not have a readily willing partner. This "problem" was the birth of prostitution, which has claimed to be the world's oldest profession. Current social standards and a sense of morality in our culture have lead to the rejection of prostitution. It has been cast it aside as a deviant behavior by the prostitute and the client. This sense of a moral code led to the development of the black tie affair.

During the Great Depression the nature of prostitution changed. The gulf between rich and poor widened and men across the nation were out of work. When it fell upon their wives and girlfriends to support the family, a great number of them turned to prostitution. The usage of prostitutes by wealthy clientele was commonplace but still frowned upon. It was because of this condemnation that patrons began disguising prostitutes in fancy clothing and taking them to gala events (this is also thought to be the beginning of the escort business) to save face socially, and then engaging in coitus.

blind Hou·di·ni, n.

1. American magician known for his escapes from chains, handcuffs, strait-jackets, and padlocked containers. Having a maximal visual acuity of the better eye, after correction by refractive lenses, of one-tenth normal vision or less.

2. United States magician (born in Hungary), famous for his ability to escape from chains or handcuffs or straitjackets or padlocked containers, who performed by instruments and without the use of sight.

3. A sexual act that occurs during coitus in the "doggy style" position when the male initiator expectorates (often with a degree of showmanship) upon the back of the recipient, thereby creating the illusion of ejaculation. When the recipient turns around, the male (a.k.a. the magician) ejaculates in the eyes of the recipient, rendering them temporarily sightless.

Middle English, from Old English. See *bhel-1* in Indo-European roots; and "escape artist or other ingenious person," 1923, from Harry *Houdini,* professional name of U.S. escape artist Erich Weiss (1874–1926).

EX. Theodore went to see the performance of the famous *blind Houdini.*

The *blind Houdini,* much like famed magician Harry Houdini, relies simply on diversion, misdirection, and an impeccable sense of timing. Later in his life, the magician took it upon himself to debunk spiritualists, who claimed possession of second sight. The blind Houdini also serves to literally blind the recipient with ejaculate entering and covering the eyes, thereby rendering the subject temporarily blind. Although not popular until after his death, the blind Houdini follows the format of many of Houdini's magic tricks, many of which were later enumerated in his book *Houdini on Magic.* Like many euphemisms, this one conflates male power and virility by likening semen and ejaculation not just to magic, but to one of the greatest magicians the world has seen. The blind Houdini embodies the subjugation of women typically found in a majority of euphemisms. It even goes as far as to suggest that one would enjoy, and be impressed by, a simple well-aimed ejaculation.

Blind Houdini, n.

box lunch at the "Y", n.

1. An individual portion of lunch packed in a small box, generally to be con-
   sumed at the community organization YMCA (Young Men's Christian
   Association). YMCA is often further abbreviated as the "Y."

2. Cunnilingus. (slang)

Middle English, from Old English, from Late Latin *buxis,* from Greek *puxis,*
from *puxos;* box tree combined with the Old English *luncheon,* shortened to
lunch, both being modified by the modern abbreviation for YMCA first
recorded as the "Y" in 1915.

EX. Every day, Carrie was hungry so her mother would always pack her a small
lunch. Carrie would have her *box lunch at the "Y."*

The origins of *box lunch at the "Y"* are rooted in several other euphemisms.
Starting in the late eighteenth century (most likely in southern England), the
vagina came to be referred to as the "box." The development of the euphemism had a twofold origin. First, the vagina was referred to as the box because,
even among the serf population, it was considered inappropriate to directly refer to a woman's reproductive organs due to the mythical power that they ap-
parently possessed (generally rooted in their purported lack of cleanliness and
shame created by the Church at the time). Secondly, and more obviously, because one is capable of inserting things into a box, and one is also capable of
inserting things into a vagina. Simply paired with lunch box, would alone imply cunnilingus, but the addition of "Y" (due to the shape of the vagina, including pubic hair, which when a women is standing standing resembles the
capital letter *Y*) makes the euphemism twice as referential to cunnilingus, almost as a double entendre.

Box lunch at the "Y", n.

brown mush·room, n.

1. Any of various fleshy fungi of the class Basidiomycota, characteristically having an umbrella-shaped cap borne on a stalk; especially any of the edible kinds, as those of the genus Agaricus, of or having the color brown.

2. A specific sexual act involving the removal of the penis from the anal canal and proceeding to strike the recipient's forehead with the penis, thereby leaving a brown stain on the forehead comprised of the recipient's feces. (slang)

Middle English, from Old English *brn.* See *bher* in Indo-European roots; and the alteration (influenced by room) of Middle English *musheron,* from Anglo-Norman *moscheron, musherum,* from Old French *mousseron,* from Medieval Latin *musari, musarin-.*

EX. Jared had to run to the store because his recipe for stirfry called for a shiitake, which is a common *brown mushroom.*

The *brown mushroom* is one of the more modern euphemisms to enter into laymen's speech. It is part of a category that is quite nontraditional in the sense that the references in these euphemisms are not a disguise for common sexual acts but are euphemisms for very specific acts that involve sex or other specialized sexual activities. The origin of brown mushroom stems from the use of the penis as a means of transporting feces to the forehead and leaving an imprint. Although it is not realistic to expect (due to the general strength of the sphincter muscles) that an ample, even coat of feces would remain on the penis after anal intercourse, it has still asserted itself as one of the more common specialty euphemisms.

buff the ba·nan·a, v.

1. To polish or shine with a piece of soft material any of several treelike Asian herbs of the genus *Musa*, especially *Musa acuminata,* having a terminal crown of large, entire leaves and a hanging cluster of fruits.
2. To make the elongated, edible fruit of these plants, having a thick yellowish to reddish skin and white, aromatic, seedless pulp shiny by rubbing or chemical action.
3. Masturbation. (slang) (specifically male)

From obsolete *buffle, buffalo,* from French *buffle,* from Late Latin *bfalus,* modified by the Portuguese; and Spanish from Wolof, Mandingo, and Fulani.

EX. Michael saw the success that the Amish had with their glowing produce, so he decided to *buff his banana* every morning before going to the market in hopes of increasing his revenue.

The use of *buff the banana* is simple in origin. Referring to the penis as a banana is rooted in the similar shapes of the penis and the banana. Additionally, the action of buffing is similar to the repeated stroking and rubbing of the penis during masturbation. Buff the banana is one of the few euphemisms that are entirely logical and accurate in their representations of the sexual act being described.

Buff the banana, v.

bump·ing ug·lies, v.

1. To cause to knock against an obstacle that is repulsive or offensive; objectionable.
2. To strike or collide with an object that is displeasing to the eye; unsightly.
3. Coitus. (slang)

Scandanavian, probably echoic; original sense was "hitting," then of "swelling from being hit." Also has a long association with obsolete *bum*, to make a booming noise. With Middle English, frightful, repulsive, from Old Norse *uggligr,* from *uggr,* fear.

EX. Justin just came back from the optometrist and couldn't see, so he was *bumping uglies* when he went to Wal-Mart.

Bumping uglies is one of the simplest and most common euphemisms. The origin of this term dates back to the late nineteenth century when Pope Pius IX held the first Vatican Council on December 8, 1869. The term was originated by the faithful in Rome to show disgust with what they thought was the decline of morality in then contemporary Italian society, due to perceived licentious and deviant behavior brought about by unease surrounding the Franco-Prussian war. Originally coined *adesdum inhonestus* in the language of the Roman Catholic church, the term carried connotations of a corruption of morality (*inhonestus* carried with it a double meaning of ugly, implying both a physical and moral deformity) and a violent unrestrained nature. American soldiers stationed in Italy during World War I brought this euphemism home in its modern version bumpin' uglies. The tendencies of our soldiers overseas were no secret to their wives and girlfriends at home, and this euphemism spread to show distaste for their actions in our morally upright culture. The shame involved with sexual activity (especially out of wedlock) reinforced the common perception of the genitals as ugly and further aided the popularity of this euphemism.

bur·y the bone, v.

1. To conceal by or as if by covering over with earth any of numerous anatomically distinct structures making up the skeleton of a vertebrate animal.
2. To place the dense, semirigid, porous, calcified connective tissue forming the major portion of the skeleton of most vertebrate in the ground.
3. Coitus. (slang)

Middle English *burien,* from Old English *byrgan.* See *bhergh* in Indo-European Roots and Middle English *bon,* from Old English *bn.*

EX. Karen found that someone kept stealing her dog's toys, so she decided to *bury the bone* in the backyard.

The success of *bury the bone* as a euphemism in today's vernacular lies in its simplicity. The penis has been referred to as a boner, bone, or the bone since the fifteenth century. Bury the bone has a sordid history in its evolution as a sexual euphemism, theoretically involving necrophilia and grave robberies in the suburbs of London in the late seventeenth century. Its popularity today has nothing to do with its risqué past, and it relies almost totally on the simplicity of design. A common understanding of this euphemism is that the bone is a reference to the penis and it gets "buried" in the vagina. Sadly, the original context of this euphemism is almost lost due to the lack of desire to understand the etymology of our vernacular.

Bury the bone, v.

butt pi·rate, n.

1. One who robs at sea or plunders a unit of volume equal to two hogsheads (usually the equivalent of 126 U.S. gallons) from the sea without commission from a sovereign nation.

2. One who makes use of or reproduces the larger or thicker end of an object without authorization.

3. Homosexual. (slang) (specifically male) (often considered offensive)

Middle English *butte, target,* from Old French, from butt, goal, end, target. See *butt;* and Middle English, from Old French, from Latin *prta,* from Greek *peirts,* from *peirn,* to attempt, from *peira,* trial. See *per* in Indo-European roots.

EX. Samuel had been collecting his father's smoked cigarettes since he was three; he was the biggest *butt pirate* in the tristate area.

Butt pirate originated during the Spanish Inquisition. It was a derisive jeer often tossed from the bow of one ship to another, implying a weakness of skill and an inability to pirate anything of real value. The term evolved to imply the forceful taking of anal sex, although that is not often how it is used. The implications are ripe with masculine stereotypes, into assumption that no one would willingly engage in anal sex, so the act must involve piracy of some nature.

cam·el toe, n.

1. One of the digits of a humped, long-necked ruminant mammal of the genus *Camelus,* domesticated in Old World desert regions as a beast of burden and as a source of wool, milk, and meat.
2. The lowest, outermost, or endmost part of a device used to raise sunken objects, consisting of a hollow structure that is submerged, attached tightly to the object, and pumped free of water. Also called caisson.
3. A profile of the labia that is clearly visible and well defined, generally through very tight clothing. (slang)

Middle English, from Old English, and from Anglo-Norman *cameil,* both from Latin *camlus,* from Greek *kamlos;* of Semitic origin. See *gml* in Semitic root; and Middle English, from Old English. See *deik-* in Indo-European roots.

EX. While at the zoo, Allen pointed out the *camel toes* to his mother.

One of the few euphemisms brought back from travels in the Sahara Desert, *camel toe* is a very simple term. French colonists would work in missions and encounter the local wildlife. It was observed that the toes of a camel looked remarkably similar to the outer labia. Although this term started out as merely a descriptive term for the shaved labia, it has now come to signify the shape of the labia as seen through clothing, and no longer is exclusive to the bare labia.

chal·leng·er (the), n.

1. One who competes against the holder of a title or championship, as in boxing.
2. One that challenges.
3. NASA's second space shuttle orbiter to be put into service, after *Columbia.*
4. A sexual act consisting of three men simultaneously penetrating the same female. This can occur in any combination of oral, anal, and vaginal. (slang) (often considered offensive)

From 1292, Old Francophonic *chalenge*, accusation, claim, dispute, from Latin *calumnia*, trickery (see *calumny*). Accusatory connotations died out in the seventeenth century. Meaning "a calling to fight" is from 1530. *Challenged* as a euphemism for "disabled" dates from 1985.

EX. Karen and Andy went to Florida to see the launch of the *Challenger.*

One of the least tasteful euphemisms of our time is surprisingly not offensive because of what it represents, but for what it is named after. The *challenger,* an "homage" to the disaster on the morning of January 28, 1986, of the tenth mission of the space shuttle *Challenger,* is a euphemism that, like many others, pays no attention to its cultural bearing. This familiarity is often advantageous to the propagation of a euphemism regardless of its contents. The challenger almost uses the sadness and tragedy of the demise of the seven crew aboard as a warning to women of licentious character. From the press footage one can clearly see the shuttle break into three major pieces. Each of the pieces represent one active participant in the euphemism. The act of triple penetration, especially in the pornographic footage of today, is not uncommon, and making a clever name for the act (apart from the standard "triple stuff") was deemed necessary to popularize the then controversial act. This was a euphemism, much like the *money shot,* that originated on the set of the pornographic film industry.

check the oil, v.

1. A standard method of inspecting or evaluating the lubricating fluid in an automobile engine.
2. To assess the presence of a slippery, viscous, and combustible liquid used in a great variety of products, especially lubricants and fuels, by means of visual confirmation.
3. Anal sex or manual stimulation of the anus by another device or appendage. (slang)

From Middle English, from Old English *hafod.* See *kaput-* in Indo-European Root and the Middle English *chek,* check in chess, from Old French *eschec,* from Arabic *shh,* from Persian, king, *check.* See *shah,* and Middle English, from Old French *oile,* from Latin *oleum,* olive oil, from Greek *elaiwon, elaion,* from *elaiw, elai,* olive.

EX. Albert's car wasn't running right, so he decided to *check the oil.*

Although impractical and often unrealistic, *check the oil* refers to an abundance of feces remaining on any appendage after insertion into the anus. The inaccuracies in this euphemism lie in the strength of the sphincter muscles. The vast majority of feces remains in the anus after removal of the penis or finger from the anus. Check the oil is not only reference to the stimulation of the prostate or exterior walls of the vagina by entrance through the anal canal, but it also refers to a threatening act often discussed in adolescent male circles by which a finger, hand, or other object is forcibly inserted into an offending male's anus.

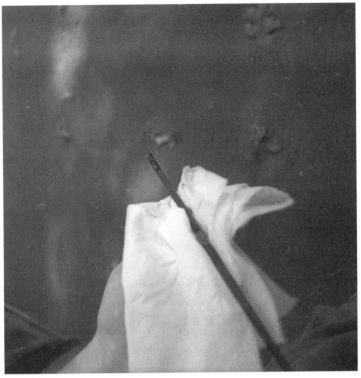

Check the oil, v.

chok·ing the chick·en, v.

1. To interfere with the respiration of common domestic fowl (*Gallus domesticus*) by compression or obstruction of the larynx or trachea.
2. To check or slow down the movement, growth, or action of any of various foolhardy competitions in which the participants persist in a dangerous course of action until one loses nerve and stops.
3. Masturbation. (slang) (specifically male)

Middle English *choken,* short for *achoken,* from Old English *cecian*: -, intensive pref. + *coce, cace,* jaw, cheek; and Old English *cycen*, young fowl, which in Middle English came to mean young chicken, then any chicken, from West Germanic *kiukinam,* from base *keuk-* (possibly root of cock, of echoic origin).

EX. Whenever Bill went out to get a chicken for his dinner, they would all run around and he could never catch one. This made him so angry that when he finally did capture one of the crafty fowl, he would *choke the chicken* before cutting off its head.

Choke the chicken originated from the French practice of choking a chicken (or breaking its neck) instead of decapitation. This practice was used to avoid the inevitable mess of beheading a chicken (and their tendency to run around afterward, necks spouting blood), and the French desire for a more acceptable method of preparing their meals. The sexual reference arose in reference to the method used by the French to hold their chickens while twisting their heads. The chicken would be placed between the knees and thighs, and the chef would stroke the neck of the chicken to coax the bird into a relaxed state and then twist the neck of the bird. When observed, this practice looks very similar to male masturbation, with the combination of the location of chicken, the gentle stroking of the elongated neck, the sharp twist, the blood spurting from the mouth of the chicken, and the satisfied countenance of the chef.

Choking the chicken, v.

Cleve·land steam·er, n.

1. A vehicle, machine, or engine driven by steam from the city with that name in northeastern Ohio on Lake Erie, which is a port of entry and industrial center.

2. A container in which something is steamed that has been manufactured in Cleveland, a city and major port in northeastern Ohio.

3. A clam from Lake Erie fished out of the waters near the Bass Islands that is usually steamed in the shell.

4. A sexual act whereby the active participant defecates upon the chest of the recipient and then proceeds to sit upon the feces and rock back and forth.

Old English from Middle English *steam*, vapor, fume, from Pre-Germanic *stau-maz* (cf. Du. *stoom*), of unknown origin. The verb is from Old English *stemen, stymen*, to emit a scent or odor; slang meaning "to make angry" is from 1922. *Steamy* is first noted in 1644; in the sense of "erotic, sexy," it is first recorded 1952 and early Anglian dialect *cliver*, expert at seizing, probably from E.Fris. *klufer* or Norwegian dialectic *klover*, ready, skillful, perhaps influenced by Old English *clifer*, claw, hand.

EX. Annie worked as a chef at Le Grande Cherie and they had a *Cleveland steamer* for their potatoes.

The *Cleveland steamer* is one of the more culturally and geographically specific euphemisms. In Cleveland, a massive amount of clear cutting and tree processing for paper, as well as the steel industry, left the city riddled with pollution and a distinct odor. Visitors would often leave "steamy Cleveland" and bring with them tales of rapid development, the resulting stench, and Cleveland's new nickname, "Steamy Cleveland." After the Cuyahoga River caught fire in 1969 and the pollution of the city was more than just a citywide joke, the term Cleveland steamer was born. The implications of pollution and excessive waste inherent in any scatological act was easily attached to Cleveland's old nickname steamy Cleveland, and the "processing" of said waste by the rocking motions of a steamroller were a nod to the effects of Cleveland's industrial problems. The late acceptance of this euphemism into American slang was largely due to the oddity and seemingly infrequent real-life usage of the act of compression of feces on one's chest as a sexual act, but its wit and humor prevailed in the mid-1980s, when the Cleveland steamer entered our vernacular.

cock jock·ey, n.

1. One who rides an adult male chicken in races, especially as a profession.
2. To direct or maneuver domesticated male fowl by cleverness or skill.
3. Homosexual. (slang) (specifically male) (often considered offensive)
4. Any person or persons engaging in sexual intercourse. (slang)

Middle English *cok*, from Old English *cocc*, probably from Late Latin *coccus*, from *coco,* a cackling, of imitative origin certain connection with cock, but Germanic has *hahn*, hen, in many of the same senses and diminutive of Scots Jock, variant of Jack. From the name Jack, from Middle English Jakke, possibly from Old French Jacques, from Late Latin Iacbus, and Middle English, from Old French Jehan, from Late Latin Ioannes, Iohannes, from Greek Ianns, from Hebrew *yônn,* Yahweh has been gracious: *yô,* Yahweh; see *hwy* in Semitic roots + *nan,* he has been gracious; see *nn* in Semitic roots.

EX. Dennis went to the races on the weekends and always put his money on Gerald Weathertree, his favorite *cock jockey,* and his mount, Foghorn Leghorn.

Cock jockey is one of the few truly American euphemisms. It came to popularity in the Revolutionary War as a pejorative term for the British infantry. It was a mockery of British culture and British men, which the American troops saw as emasculated, and altogether too fancy, an idea that often carries over in today's assumptions of the British. It was meant to imply two things: first, the short stature of the British soldiers (although they were no smaller than the American troops); and second, to call into question their sexuality and imply that while away from home they engaged in sexual congress within the ranks of the military.

dirt·y san·chez, n.

1. A Venezuelan master terrorist raised by a Marxist-Leninist father; he trained and worked with many terrorist groups, apt to soil with dirt or grime.

2. Any person or persons called Sanchez who are soiled, as with dirt or are generally unclean.

3. A sexual act in which the active participant inserts his/her finger into the anus of the recipient in order to coat the finger with feces and then proceeds to spread the feces onto the recipients upper lip in the shape of a curled mustache. (slang) (often considered offensive)

Old English *salo*, dusky, dark (related to *sol*, dark, dirty), from Pre-Germanic. *salwa-* (cf. Middle Dutch, *salu*, discolored, dirty, Old High German *salo*, dirty gray, Old Norse *sölr*, dirty yellow), from PIE base *sal-*, dirty, gray (cf. Old Church Slavonic *slavojocije*, grayish blue color, Russian *solovoj*, cream-colored); and Sanchez of Indo-European and Vulgar Latin roots.

EX. When Galo met Sanchez after work, he exclaimed, "That is one *dirty Sanchez!*"

Coined in Texas in the late 1860s, the *dirty sanchez* was the product of the Mexican-American War that raged from 1846–48. When a Mexican soldier was captured, American soldiers would often wipe themselves with their hand and rub a mixture of sweat and fecal matter under the nose of the captured Mexican soldier. The use of *dirty* in the euphemism carries cultural and racial implications as well. Americans at the time saw the residents of Mexico as backwards, poor, dirty, almost subhuman. It is no surprise that when reducing Mexicans to a single cultural trait, exaggerated versions of this simple facial hairstyle were linked to the public's perception of Mexican laziness, ineptitude, stupidity, and inferiority. While the original dirty sanchez was a dehumanizing tactic of a gruesome war, the contemporary euphemism has expanded to adopt some of the cultural associations attached to the Mexican laborer/soldier, primarily the exaggerated moustache. The performance of a contemporary dirty sanchez involves many of the same aspects of the original, but as sanitation practices have improved, it is now necessary to insert a finger into the anus of either participant in the dirty sanchez in order to have adequate feces and control to draw the exaggerated (and curled) Mexican moustache on the upper lip of the recipient.

Dirty sanchez, n.

don·key punch, v.

1. To hit the domesticated ass (*Equus asinus*) with a sharp blow of the fist.
2. To hit with a quick short swing a domesticated hoofed mammal of the horse family with long ears and a braying call.
3. A sexual act involving striking the recipient in the small of the back during intercourse (anal or vaginal) in order to force the contraction of pubic and lower back muscles. (slang)

1785, slang, perhaps from *dun,* dull gray-brown, the form perhaps influenced by monkey. Or possibly from a familiar form of *Duncan* (cf. *dobbin*). The older English word was ass; and Middle English *punchen,* to thrust, prod, prick, from Old French *poinçonner, ponchonner,* to emboss with a punch, from *poinçon, ponchon,* pointed tool. See puncheon.

EX. Kevin had a donkey on his farm that was acting up, he decided to give him the old *donkey punch* to keep his animal in line.

The *donkey punch* is one of the most unique euphemisms of our time. It falls into the class of theoretical euphemisms that are infrequent, impractical, and violent. The almost purely theoretical nature of the donkey punch makes it one of the most informative euphemisms about contemporary American society. The donkey punch originated in the late twentieth century sometime after the sexual revolution, when the empowerment of women was threatening the place of men in contemporary society. This shift in gender paradigms left men feeling threatened, and to reassert their authority, they created and popularized these theoretical and violent euphemisms. The effectiveness of the donkey punch rests in the reaction of the female recipient (or homosexual male in rare cases), being similar to a donkey in the bray and kick after getting punched in the small of the back. The primary "reward" for the initiator of the donkey punch is the tensing of the vaginal (or anal) muscles immediately prior to ejaculation, which serves to intensify the orgasm of the male. The secondary reward of the donkey punch is the creation, or reinforcement, of the ideal power structure or solidifying existing gender roles.

Ex·xon Val·dez, n.

1. The original name of an oil tanker owned by the Exxon oil company. The ship was renamed the *Sea River Mediterranean* after the March 24, 1989, oil spill in which the tanker hit Prince William Sound's Bligh Reef.

2. A premeditated act whereby the female perforates her diaphragm and uses petroleum jelly instead of spermicidal jelly in order to increase the chances of insemination, without the knowledge or consent of her male counterpart. (slang)

Contrived by Esso (Standard Oil of New Jersey) in the early 1970s to create a neutral but distinctive label for the company. Within days of announcement of the name, Exxon was being called the "double cross company" but this eventually subsided. (Esso is a trademark of ExxonMobil.) Esso had to change its name for American purposes to Exxon because of restrictions dating to the 1911 Standard Oil antitrust decision and Valdez, surname of Hispanic origin and a port in Alaska.

EX. Sean volunteered to help clean up the massive environmental damage caused by the wreck of the *Exxon Valdez*.

The *Exxon Valdez* is a euphemism that follows the course of its namesake, which on March 24, 1989, leaked an estimated 10.8 million gallons of oil (nearly one-sixth of its full payload) into Prince William Sound. The damage caused by this fraction of the tanker's capacity had devastating effects on the environment. There are several reasons why this euphemism came to symbolize the often-devious sabotage of contraception. Referencing the hole that caused the leak in the tanker, the euphemism is applied to the actions of a woman creating a hole in the diaphragm in order to allow sperm to pass unhindered. The recommended usage of a diaphragm involves the use of a spermicidal jelly; this detergent-based lubricant/spermicide is the last line of defense should semen enter the cervical canal or bypass the barrier created by the diaphragm. Ironically, to perform the Exxon Valdez, the female replaces the customary spermicide with petroleum jelly. If a condom is used in addition to the diaphragm, the petroleum serves to break this final barrier to semen, as latex weakens in the presence of petroleum-based lubricants—making the final corrupting element in the Exxon Valdez none other than a by-product of what the infamous vessel contained.

five a·gainst one, v.

1. The cardinal number equal to 4 + 1 in opposition to or on a course opposite to a single entity, unit, object, or living being.

2. Something, such as a quintet or a basketball team, that has five parts, units, or members in hostile opposition or resistance to the single member or element of a group.

3. Male masturbation. (slang)

Middle English, from Old English *ff.* See *penkwe* in Indo-European roots; Middle English, alteration of *againes,* from Old English *ongeagn*; and Middle English *on,* from Old English *n.* See *oi-no- in* Indo-European roots.

EX. Roger and his friends went to the park to get a pick-up game of basketball going, but someone was on the court playing a game of *five against one.*

Ironically, *five against one* is rooted in literature. It was first introduced to the mainstream by Ernest Hemingway in his seminal novel, *A Farewell to Arms**, "priest every night five against one." The use of this witty turn of phrase is rooted in the number of fingers on a hand (used for masturbation) and the single appendage of male sexuality—five fingers against one penis. The term *against* implies a certain aggressiveness and confrontation common to many sexual euphemisms involving male masturbation; in order to make masturbation seem less shameful and more masculine, it has been given these terms that imply power and domination.

---

* Ernest Hemingway. *A Farewell to Arms,* (New York: Scribner paperback, reprint, 1995; original publication 1929) page 7.

flick the bean, v.

1. Touch or hit any of various New World twining herbs of the genus *Phaseolus* in the pea family with a light quick blow.
2. To cause a seed or pod of any of these plants to move with a quick blow.
3. Female masturbation. (slang)

From *flycke c.* 1447, probably imitative of a light blow with a whip. Earliest recorded use is in phrase "not worth a flykke," useless; and Middle English *ben,* broad bean, from Old English *ban.* See *bha-bh-* in Indo-European roots.

EX. Sarah was a troublemaker and she would *flick the bean* across the cafeteria during the majority of her lunch hour.

Flick the bean is one of many euphemisms that have anatomical origins. The clitoris has been referred to as the bean for almost three centuries due to its size and shape. The use of the word flick in this euphemism is an obvious reference to the hand motion in the stimulation of the clitoris. Although not an exciting euphemism in origin, flick the bean is one of the most common euphemisms for female masturbation.

Flick the bean, v.

fudge pack·er, n.

1. One whose profession is to process and put into containers in order to preserve, transport, or sell a soft rich candy made of sugar, milk, butter, and flavoring.

2. One who presses together or compacts firmly rich chocolate used especially in cakes or as a sauce on ice cream.

3. Homosexual. (slang) (often considered offensive)

Possibly alteration of *fadge,* to fit; and Middle English *pak,* possibly of Low German origin.

EX. Mark worked at Aunt Mamie's Confectionary as a *fudge packer.*

The *fudge packer* is one of the few euphemisms that is almost literal in nature and gives little clues to the society that spawned it. Fudge packer is one of the simplest references to anal sex in the contemporary American language. Interestingly, there is little derisiveness inherent in the euphemism and any derogatory slant that this term takes on is almost entirely based in connotation of the speaker. As a term that refers primarily to homosexual men, it is remarkable that no subtle innuendo or any contemptuous subtext exists. The fudge packer is simply a reference to the repeated plunging of the penis into the colon, whereby feces are compacted and so made more dense.

fuzz·y dough·nut (also do·nut), n.

1. A small sugar-coated cake of sweet dough, either fried or baked, spherical with a filling of cream or jam or ring-shaped with no filling, and covered with a mass of short fine hairs or fibers.

2. An object in the shape of an inflated ring, for example, an accelerating tube in a nuclear reactor, or an undersized spare tire in the form of a mass of short fine hairs or fibers.

3. Labia. (slang)

Perhaps from Low German *fussig,* spongy. See *p-* in Indo-European roots; and American English, from dough + nut. First recorded by Washington Irving in 1809, who described them as "balls of sweetened dough, fried in hog's fat, and called doughnuts, or olykoeks."

EX. Sam was very disappointed when he dropped his sweet breakfast treat on the carpet, and exclaimed "Damn it, now all I have is a *fuzzy donut.*"

The origins of *fuzzy donut* spring from the use of donut as a euphemism for the labia in the mid-twentieth century in middle America. The addition of fuzzy suggests the texture of the labia (as donut functions as a descriptor of the shape) and completes the euphemism as an approximation of the labia in size and shape.

George Wal·ker, n.

1. 43rd President of the United States; son of former president George Herbert Walker Bush.
2. One that walks, especially a contestant in a footrace whose name is George.
3. A predisposition to anal intercourse or any anal activity that borders on obsession. (slang)

Middle English *walken,* from Old English *wealcan,* to roll. See *wel*-2 in Indo-European roots and Old English *wealcan*, to toss, roll, and *wealcian* to roll up, curl, muffle up, from Pre-Germanic *welk-* (cf. Old Norse *valka*, to drag about, Danish *valke*, to full, Middle Dutch *walken*, to knead, press, full, Old High German *walchan*, to knead, Germanic *walken*, to full), perhaps ult. from PIE base *wel-*, to turn, bend, twist, roll (see vulva). Meaning shifted in early Middle English, perhaps from colloquial use of the Old English word.

Ex. As the forty-third president of the United States of America, *George Walker* Bush invaded Iraq to control the oil supplies in the Middle East.

The *George Walker* (sometimes referred to as the "Dubya") is one of the newest euphemisms to gain a foothold in American culture. Modeled after its namesake's endless pursuit of oil (seemingly at any cost), the George Walker is similarly the pursuit of anal intercourse (represented by oil) at any cost. This can be achieved by manipulation of a semi-willing participant, paying a prostitute a premium fee, and even sometimes by force. The dropping of the surname Bush from the euphemism is a further reference to the preference of anal over vaginal intercourse (the vagina is commonly referred to as the "bush") and the refusal to seek alternate means of sexual gratification. Popularized in 2003, the George Walker stemmed from public outrage surrounding the preemptive strike on Iraq. Originally used only to describe forced anal intercourse (primarily in prisons), the euphemism was so popular that the usage naturally expanded to encompass any predisposition to anal intercourse. The political slant and general disapproval of the forty-third president of the United States have made this euphemism one of the more popular in our time.

get·ting head, v.

1. To come into possession or use of the uppermost or forward most part of the body of a vertebrate, containing the brain and the eyes, ears, nose, mouth, and jaws.
2. To go after and bring the mythical seat of the faculty of reason, intelligence, intellect, or mind.
3. Fellatio. (slang)

From Middle English *geten*, from Old Norse *geta*. See *ghend-* in Indo-European roots; and the Middle English, from Old English *hafod*. See *kaput-* in Indo-European roots.

EX. Joanne was quite excited because this birthday, much like her previous twenty, she was *getting head* to add to her collection.

The term *getting head* originated from the action of the head while performing fellatio. Traditionally, there is a misconception regarding the difference between fellatio and irrumatio. The subtle difference between these two terms originates from the difference in style of the performing of oral sex on the male. Irrumatio is an act where the mouth and throat (male or female) act as a receptacle for the thrusting penis (the mouth and throat being passive recipients). With fellatio (as in getting head), the mouth is the active participant often bobbing up and down on the penis. This bobbing action as perceived by the male recipient is interpreted as getting head due to the "receiving" of oral sex and the motion of the head occupying the majority of the field of view.

Getting head, v.

glaz·ing the dough·nut (also do·nut), v.

1. To apply a glaze to a small, ring-shaped cake made of rich, light dough that is deep fried in fat.
2. To give a smooth lustrous surface to something whose form is reminiscent of a ring-shaped cake.
3. Coitus. (slang)
4. Expelling semen on or around the labia or anus. (slang)

From Middle English *glasen,* from *glas,* glass, from Old English *glæs.* See *ghel* in Indo-European roots and American English, from dough + nut. First recorded by Washington Irving in 1809, who described them as "balls of sweetened dough, fried in hog's fat, and called doughnuts, or olykoeks."

EX. Samuel wanted to get some food at the donut shop, but Suzy was in the back *glazing the donut,* and her hands were too sticky to work the register.

Glazing the donut refers to coitus (primarily) or the expelling of semen onto the anus or vagina (second). The use of donut originated from the approximate shape of the vagina and anus. The use of the term as a descriptor of coitus ignores the practical and literal use of the euphemism. The vagina (see *fuzzy donut*) is commonly referred to in this euphemism, but given proportional shape, the anus is a more logical choice.

Glazing the doughnut (also donut), v.

hang·ing john·ny, v.

1. A loose short-sleeved gown opening in the back, worn by patients undergoing medical treatment or examination, which has been placed on a hook.
2. Execution by hanging on a gallows of any person named Johnny.
3. Male masturbation. (slang)

Middle English *hongen*, from Old English *hangian*, to be suspended, and from *hn*, to hang. See *konk-* in Indo-European roots; and masculine proper name, c.1160, from Medieval Latin Johannes, from Late Latin Joannes, from Greek Ioannes, from Hebrew Yohanan (in full, *y'hohanan*), literally "Jehovah has favored," from *hanan*, "he was gracious."

EX. Beatrice was heartbroken to find out that the posse had finally caught up with her husband and was *hanging Johnny* for cheating at cards.

Hanging johnny is another of the euphemisms for male masturbation that involves violence. As noted in the definition of *donkey punch*, contemporary masculinity has developed the need to have all aspects of sexual activity be a power-seeking event for men. Even when the male is the only person involved, it is about a domination of his penis. Hanging Johnny originated from the grip often used on the penis (which is often referred to as Johnny) while masturbating, which can easily resemble choking or hanging.

hide the sa·la·mi, v.

1. To put or keep out of sight any of a variety of highly spiced and salted sausages, made from beef or a mixture of pork and beef.
2. To prevent the disclosure or recognition of highly seasoned fatty sausages of pork or beef.
3. Coitus. (slang)

Middle English, from Old English *hd.* See *kei* in Indo-European roots; and Italian, plural of *salame, salami,* from Vulgar Latin *salmen,* from *salre,* to salt, from Latin *sl,* salt. See *sal-* in Indo-European roots.

EX. Maggie's fat uncle Charles was coming over, so she had to *hide the salami* before he arrived.

Hide the salami has roots in the old German game capture the flag. The American soldiers overseas in World War II would frequent German brothels (or brothels staffed by German expatriate prostitutes) and copulate with the German prostitutes. This led to talk among the ranks of what activities transpired, and not wanting to be berated by their commanding officers for commiserating with the enemy they would talk about playing a game of hide the salami, which was a stab at the sausage-loving German people.

Hide the salami, v.

hot meat (also beef) in·jec·tion, n.

1. The results of the act or process of filling vessels, cavities, or tissues with the edible flesh of animals, especially mammals, that has or is giving off heat.
2. The edible fleshy tissue of mammals, being at a high temperature, that is forced or driven, especially as a dose of liquid medicine injected, into the body.
3. Coitus. (slang)

Middle English, from Old English *ht*. See *kai-* in Indo-European roots, Middle English *mete,* from Old English, *food;* and Latin *inicere, iniect-,* to throw in : *in-,* in; see *in, iacere,* to throw; see *y-* in Indo-European roots.

EX. Joan was so emaciated from her anorexia that when she got to the hospital, the doctor had to give her a *hot meat injection* just so she could begin to regain her strength.

Contrary to popular belief, *hot meat injection* has little to do with the age-old reference to the penis as the meat. The popularity of the hot meat injection is actually rooted in the polio vaccine developed by Jonas Salk on April 12, 1955. Although the development of the polio vaccine did not start the term, it did gain massive popularity as polio ravaged Europe. It was a running joke that as Salk's vaccine was the cure for polio, the hot meat injection was the cure to the rest of life's problems. The hot meat injection is another of the euphemisms that reference the preciousness of the penis by comparison of the penis to medicine.

in·spec·tor of man·holes, n.

1. One who is appointed or employed to inspect a hole, usually with a cover, through which a person may enter a sewer, boiler, drain, or similar structure.

2. Homosexual. (slang) (specifically male) (often considered offensive)

Old French, *inspection*, from Latin *inspectionem* (nominitive, *inspectio*), a looking into, from *inspectus*, past participle of *inspicere*, look into, inspect, examine, from *in-*, into, and *specere*, to look. Inspector, meaning overseer or superintendent, is from 1602; as a police ranking between sergeant and superintendent, it dates from 1840. Old English from *mann* and *hol,* orifice, hollow place.

EX. Reginald was always a diligent student. When he graduated from technical school, he was hired by the city as an *inspector of manholes*.

Inspector of manholes falls into a group of euphemisms known as the "double entendre." Euphemisms of this category are liable to more than one interpretation. This simple euphemism uses a common word in society (manholes) and splits it up into its two parts, man and hole. Here manhole is quite literally used to describe a hole in a man, his anus (manhole also implies that said hole is intended for entrance). Inspector is now part of a logical progression in describing someone who takes great interest in the male anus.

Inspector of manholes, n.

jazz in the park, n.

1. A style of music, native to America, characterized by a strong but flexible rhythmic understructure with solo and ensemble improvisations on basic tunes and chord patterns and, more recently, a highly sophisticated harmonic idiom preformed in or around an area of land set aside for public use.

2. Big band dance music intended for performance in or on a piece of land with few or no buildings, or a piece of land adjoining a town, maintained for recreational and ornamental purposes.

3. The result of the male ejaculating on or about the pubis mons of the female recipient. (slang)

From Middle English, game preserve, enclosed tract of land, from Old French *parc,* of Germanic origin and jazz, origins unknown.

EX. Ann and George went out every Thursday in summertime to see the *jazz in the park.*

Although a simple euphemism, *jazz in the park* is not lacking in subtlety. Like many euphemisms of this type it relies on linguistic and phonetic similarities to camouflage its message. The pubis mons (often referred to as the "bush") is seen here as the park, a sprawling stretch of growth for the public enjoyment (which also carries implications about the woman involved in the act). Jazz is simply a reference to jizz or jizzum—common slang for the male ejaculate. The pairing of jazz and park is a reference to the performative aspects of the male ejaculation and the denigration of the female to the platform (or stage) of said performance.

knuck·le shuf·fle, v.

1. To move the dorsal aspect of a joint of a finger, especially of one of the joints connecting the fingers to the hand, from one place to another.
2. To slide the rounded protuberance formed by the bones in a joint along the floor or ground while walking.
3. Male masturbation. (slang)

Middle English *knokel, knokel,* finger joint, common Germanic (cf. Mid-Late Germanic *knökel,* Middle Dutch, *cnockel.* Germanic *knöchel*), literally little bone, a diminutive of Pre-Germanic root *knuck-* "bone" (cf. Germanic *Knochen,* bone); and Middle English *shovelen,* perhaps from Low Germanic *schuffeln* to walk clumsily, probably of Middle Dutch or Middle Low German origin.

EX. Anna was impressed when she got to the sock hop because she saw Ryan doing the *knuckle shuffle.*

The *knuckle shuffle* was a term made popular in the early fifties when dance nomenclature was on the rise. Soon, enterprising young men began to refer to masturbation as the knuckle shuffle as a reflection of hand and knuckle movement during masturbation (primarily as a reference to the movement of the knuckles during the stimulation of the frenulum) and general stimulation of the penis. The knuckle shuffle is a simple euphemism, and almost an anomaly in its unbiased (lacking preciousness or power) reference to male masturbation.

lay some pipe (also lay·ing pipe), v.

1. To cause an unspecified number or quantity of hollow cylinder or tube used to conduct liquid or gas to lie down.
2. To put or set down a considerable number or quantity of sections or pieces of tube used to conduct liquid.
3. Coitus. (slang)

Middle English *leien*, from Old English *lecgan*. See *legh-* in Indo-European roots; Middle English *-som,* from Old English *-sum, -like*. See *sem-1* in Indo-European roots; and Middle English, from Old English *ppe,* from Vulgar Latin *ppa,* from Latin *ppre,* to chirp.

EX. Sue called in a plumber to lay some pipe in her house because she had some leaks.

A derivation of "French kiss," through the usage of a French drain on the foundation of a house to keep water from seeping into the basement or weakening the foundation, *lay some pipe* resides in the family of euphuisms that glorify the penis and imply that intercourse is a necessity. The transformation of a French drain to lay some pipe is rooted in the physical construction of a French drain, which is constructed by placing perforated pipe at the bottom of a ditch and covering it with layers of gravel to aid drainage and keep particulates out of the pipe. In a properly made French drain (which is a standard feature in the construction of most houses), the pipe is the crucial element because carries the water away from the house and to its given destination. Hence, the first step in creating a solid home is laying some pipe for the French drain.

lit·tle Dutch boy, n.

1. A male child of small stature of or from the Netherlands.
2. A small or diminutive male child who hails from the region of Europe formerly a British colony, which was formed as the independent monarchy known as the Netherlands in 1654.
3. A sexual act whereby the male ejaculate is quickly spread over the skin to cause an even distribution. (slang)

Middle English, from Old English *ltel,* Middle English *Duch,* German, Dutch, from Middle Dutch *Dtsch.* See *teut-* in Indo-European roots; and Middle English *boi,* possibly from Old French *embuié,* servant, past participle of *embuier,* to fetter.

EX. Elizabeth tugged on her mother's shirt while exclaiming, "Look at the funny wooden shoes on that *little Dutch boy,* Mom!"

The *little Dutch boy* began as a reference to the spreading of semen in a manner that reflected the spreading of paint. This euphemism gained clout in the vernacular of euphemisms in the middle of the twentieth century as Dutch Boy brand paints increased in popularity and began to compete with their longtime rival Porter Paints. The sexual act entails spreading expelled semen around the skin of the person who was engaged in sexual congress with the instigator of the little Dutch boy. It began as an ironic act of consideration so the recipient did not need to wipe him- or herself after the sexual activity was over. Ironically, this term gained its usage not based on the act itself, but based on the laughable nature of the fact that spreading ejaculate on and around someone's skin could be seen as an act of kindness.

lit·tle red rid·ing hood, n.

1. "Little Red Riding Hood" is a popular children's fable penned by Charles Perrault in *Histoires ou Contes du temps passé* (1697) and popularized in America by the Brothers Grimm in the early nineteeth century.

2. A small or diminutive loose pliable covering for the head and neck of the color red, often used for the act of changing location by means of a moving mount.

3. The use of a condom specifically for engaging in sexual congress while the female is experiencing a menstrual cycle, so as to keep the penis free from blood or menstrual discharge. (slang)

Middle English, from Old English *ltel,* Middle English, from Old English *rad.* See *reudh-* in Indo-European roots; Middle English, alteration of *trithing,* from Old English *thrithing,* from Old Norse *thridhjungr,* third part, from *thridhi,* third. See *trei-* in Indo-European roots; and Middle English *-hed, -hode,* from Old English *-hdu, -hd.*

EX. Katie was scared, so her mother read her *Little Red Riding Hood* while she was falling asleep.

Little Red Riding Hood is a fable that many critics believe is ripe with references to sexual intercourse and violence. The use of this term as a very specific descriptor of a prophylactic used during menstruation gained popularity when literary critics began to accept old theories of sexual overtones in the original publication of the classic children's fable. The use of the title was a simple progression that combined several euphemisms. *Hood* was commonly used as a word for the male condom, *riding* had been used for centuries as a reference to the female on top position of sexual intercourse, and *red* as the color of menstrual discharge. These elements combined make an extremely logical, although bizarre, euphemism that has been common in North American vocabulary since the early 1900s.

Little red riding hood, n.

mak·in' ba·con, v.

1. To form the salted and smoked meat from the back and sides of a pig.
2. To cook or prepare salted and smoked meat from the back and sides of a pig by heating.
3. Coitus. (slang)

Middle English *maken,* from Old English *macian.* See *mag-* in Indo-European roots and *bac,* Middle English, from Old French, of Germanic origin.

EX. When Ian stopped by to see his friend Becky, she was in the kitchen *makin' bacon.*

Makin' bacon is a term that formerly carried with it connotations of an over-weight status. Excessively corpulent people were commonly referred to as fat pigs, or simply pigs. This descriptor combined with the heat and friction of sex gave rise to the concept of makin' bacon (by the heating of pork meat) and the insulting sexual euphemism. A more modern interpretation stems from the term *porking,* which is a standard euphemism for sexual intercourse. Giving reference to pork, and add to it heat (in the form of friction), makin' bacon evolved to fit more snugly in the parlance of our times.

meat in the mouth, n.

1. A sexual act whereby the male genetalia is sucked by the mouth.

2. A blow job

ex. Emily was nervous about the state of her relationship with her boyfriend, when she was caught with someone else's meat in her mouth.

Makin' bacon, v.

milk·ing the snake, v.

1. To draw milk from the teat or udder of any of numerous scaly, legless, sometimes venomous reptiles of the suborder Serpentes or Ophidia (order Squamata), having a long, tapering, cylindrical body and found in most tropical and temperate regions.
2. A method of extracting poison from a venomous snake used in the southern regions of Thailand and surrounding areas whereby the poison is used to make an antidote.
3. Male masturbation. (slang)

Middle English, from Old English *milc.* See *melg-* in Indo-European roots; and Middle English, from Old English *snaca.*

EX. On a recent trip to Chang Mai, Jake witnessed a local man *milking the snake* to make an antidote.

Milking the snake, as the second definition implies, is rooted in the activity of squeezing a snake until a milky white fluid is excreted from the snake's fangs. This action is so similar in form to some male masturbation techniques that it evolved rapidly into a sexual euphemism. In no way a stretch of logic or imagination, the snake is a clear reference to the shape (and implied innate power) of the penis, and the milk is analogous to semen. This is another of the violent, controlling, and powerful euphemisms for male masturbation, designed to enhance the mythical power of the penis.

Mo·by Dick, n.

1. The great white whale in Herman Melville's novel *Moby-Dick*; by extension, anything large and impressive.

2. A title of address (never of third-person reference), usually used to show admiration, respect, and/or friendliness to a competent hacker having the name Richard.

3. An act that occurs after ejaculation, when the male prophylactic explodes due to the girth of the penis, spilling semen out of the condom into the cervix, onto the floor, etc.

From "order of marine mammals containing whales," 1830, Modern Latin, from Latin *cetus,* from Greek *ketos* "a whale." Hence *cetology,* the study of whales, and fellow, lad, man, 1553, rhyming nickname for Rick, short for Richard, one of the commonest English names, it has long been a synonym for *fellow,* and so most of the slang senses are probably very old, but it is hard to find in surviving records. The meaning *penis* dates from 1891 in British army slang; *dickhead,* meaning *stupid person* is from 1969. Dick, meaning *detective,* has a first usage in 1908, perhaps as a shortened variant of detective.

EX. When Sarah was a little girl, her favorite book was *Moby-Dick.*

The *Moby Dick* is one of the most layered and intellectually subtle, yet intuitively obvious, euphemisms to date. Given a cursory read of Herman Melville's iconic novel of the late nineteenth century, one can easily begin to dissect the subtlety of the pervasive sexuality of the text. Moby Dick, the very subject of Melville's novel, is the father (so to speak) of this euphemism for many reasons. The similarities between the whale and the male perception of their sexual power and prowess fueled the fire for the spread of this euphemism. Moby Dick was a huge white sperm whale that bursted through a vessel (intended to contain seamen) and spilled them about the ocean. Given this selective synopsis it is not difficult to see how the euphemism arose. The whale, representing the penis, was massive, powerful, and the obsessive passion of another man. Ironically, this euphemism, like many others that tout male prowess and power, has a subtle undercurrent of homoeroticism (arguably less subtle than most).

The euphemism represents the raw unbridled animal power and dangerous size that men like to attribute to their penises. The image of a penis too massive and powerful to be contained by an invention of man (contrary of course to the wishes of nature), breaking through the seemingly fragile barrier to fulfill its destiny, is one of power and virility. An unambiguous symbol of masculinity, the Moby Dick become of the most telling euphemisms being used today.

Mo·zart (the Amadeus), n.

1. Austrian composer, among the greatest and most prolific in history. Wolfgang Amadeus Mozart's over 600 works include 41 symphonies, 27 piano
   concertos, 16 operas, 19 piano sonatas, and other orchestral and chamber
   works. As a child prodigy, he toured Europe with his father (Johann
   Georg) Leopold Mozart (1719–87), the composer of a renowned violin
   method.
2. A sexual act involving vigorous sex whereby the extremely active motions
   knock off the wig of one of the parties involved. (slang)

From Amadeus derived from Latin *amare,* to love, and *Deus* God, from Spanish *mozo,* boy, servant, from Old Spanish *moço,* Middle English, from Old
French, of Germanic origin. See *kar-* in Indo-European roots; and *Wolfgang*
derived from the Germanic *wulf* meaning wolf and *gang,* meaning path.

EX. When Jenny walked into the concert hall she expressed her love of the
Mozart that was playing in the background.

The *Mozart* originated in the late 1980s after the release of *Amadeus.* It was
Mozart's raucous behavior and sexual appetite that fostered the creation of this
euphemism. It was deemed necessary to have a euphemism named after Wolfgang Amadeus Mozart due to his rock-star-like behavior in the film. The youth
culture of Chicago started using this euphemism as a sign of respect for the
somewhat timid or "classy" music (which was revolutionary in its time) and
the juxtaposition of a wild and carnal celebrity.

mon·ey shot, n.

1. The firing or discharge of a weapon, such as a gun, that is comprised of the official currency, coins, and negotiable paper notes issued by a government.

2. A small quantity of a generally alcoholic beverage often fermented, and made of assets and property considered in terms of monetary value.

3. The moment of ejaculation when captured on film, generally for pornographic video. (slang)

Middle English *moneie,* from Old French, from Latin *monta,* mint, coinage, from *Monta,* epithet of Juno, temple of Juno of Rome where money was coined; and Middle English *shoten,* from Old English *scotan.* See *skeud-* in Indo-European roots; Interjection, alteration of shit.

EX. James was in the bar with some friends celebrating their recent victory over the Mudville 9, so they decided to have a round of *money shots.*

Money shot is a term that is truly rooted in the industry of pornographic film. The moment of ejaculation is referred to as the money shot because it is a hard shot to capture (men would often ejaculate too soon or too late or in the wrong place) and is also the quintessential shot—a very valuable shot. Additionally, for many actors in pornographic film the ability to repeat orgasm is not common, so getting the shot the first time was crucial, giving it inherent value, thus the term *money shot.*

Money shot, n.

mous·tache ride, n.

1. To be carried or conveyed, as in a vehicle or on the hair growing on the human upper lip, especially when cultivated and groomed.
2. To move by way of the hair grown on the upper lip of mature human males.
3. Cunnilingus. (slang)

French *moustache,* from Italian dialectal *mustaccio,* from Medieval Greek *moustakion,* from Greek *mustax,* mustache, upper lip; and Middle English *riden,* from Old English *rdan.* See *reidh-* in Indo-European roots.

EX. Missa was at the carnival when she saw an exciting sign: it read "*Moustache Ride,* 25 cents."

The *moustache ride* is one of the more public euphemisms. It is often accompanied by the phrase "twenty five cents" or some other paltry sum of money. It is truly simple in origin with the euphemism referring to a woman riding on a moustache (i.e. on top of a man's face) as a method of cunnilingus. This euphemism originated in west Texas in the early nineteenth century when cowboys would come off the trail and go into the brothels. It was a macho way of asking to perform cunnilingus on a female without losing one's masculine pride. It has remained popular since then and crept into popular culture in movies and literature due to its subtlety and humor.

muff div·er, n.

1. One who dives in a small cylindrical fur or cloth cover, open at both ends, in which the hands are placed for warmth, thus making them a specialist in cold-water recovery.

2. One who works under water, especially one equipped with breathing apparatus and weighted clothing, usually in search of a warm tubular covering for the hands.

3. One who performs cunnilingus. (slang)

4. Lesbian. (slang) (also called sapphic or sapphist) (slang) (often considered offensive)

Dutch *mof,* from Middle Dutch *moffel,* from Old French *mofle, mitten,* from Medieval Latin *muffula,* perhaps of Germanic origin; and Italian, from Latin *dva,* goddess, feminine of *dvus,* god. See *dyeu-* in Indo-European roots.

EX. On her cruise, Loraine dropped her favorite minx muff into the bay. Her husband, Reginald, called a *muff diver* in from Wisconsin to retrieve it.

Muff diver has origins rooted in the isle of Lesbos, island of eastern Greece in the Aegean Sea near the Northwest coast of Turkey. The people of Lesbos were known for their diving prowess, lyric poetry, and their worship of the Greek goddess *Dvas* (etymology of the word *dive,* see above). Lesbos was the home of Sappho, the great lyric poet whose erotic and romantic verse embraced women as well as men. Sapphic, meaning "relating to homosexual relations between women," and the more modern term *Lesbian* (inhabitant of Lesbos) are now used to describe homosexual females. Muff diver is a direct reference to the inhabitants of Lesbos (given their acceptance of homosexuality and sea faring, diving nature). Less classically, this term also has roots in the slang muff, used by shape and texture to describe the vulva, and the action of diving (going under).

Muff diver, n.

one-eyed yo·gurt (also yo·ghurt) sling·er, n.

1. One who possesses a singular hollow structure located in bony sockets of
    the skull, functioning independently, having a lens capable of focusing
    incident light on an internal photosensitive retina from which nerve im-
    pulses are sent to the brain, whose work or business is to hurl a custard-
    like food with a tart flavor, prepared from milk curdled by bacteria,
    especially Lactobacillus bulgaricus and Streptococcus thermophilus, with,
    or as if with, a sling.

2. One whose work or business is to throw a custard like food with a tart fla-
    vor by means of flicking the wrist, who only possesses a singular organ of
    vision or light sensitivity.

3. Penis. (slang)

Middle English, from Old English *ge,* age. See *okw-* in Indo-European roots;
Turkish *yoart, yourt,* from *your,* to knead and the Middle English *slinge.*

ᴇx. Jamie was a *one-eyed yogurt slinger* so he decided to fling fistfuls of Dannon
yogurt at his house one night.

One-eyed yogurt slinger is a combination of a few common euphemisms intended to maximize effect in the description of the penis during climax. The
reference to semen (yogurt) stems from the euphemism "population yogurt,"
which possesses obvious references to the active (sometimes called live) cultures found in yogurt. Semen is a viscous whitish secretion of the male reproductive organs, containing spermatozoa (in a sense, spermatozoa are analogous
to live cultures). The addition of one-eyed is a reference to the urethra (one eye
is common in many penis-related euphemisms), and the use of slinger is an
obvious reference to the motion of masturbation and ejaculation.

One-eyed yogurt (also yoghurt) sling·er, n.

pad·dle the pick·le, v.

1. To row a cucumber that has been preserved in brine or vinegar slowly and gently as a means of propulsion.
2. To propel a pickle by means of rhythmic, repeated rowing.
3. Male masturbation. (slang)

Middle English *padell,* tool used to clean plowshares, perhaps from Medieval Latin *padela;* and Middle English *pikle,* highly seasoned sauce, probably from Middle Dutch *pekel,* pickle, brine.

EX. Jeff was losing the pickle boat race, so he got his little arms moving and *paddled the pickle* as hard as he could to catch up with the other boys.

Paddle the pickle has always been on the fringes of the lexicon of sexual euphemisms due to the popularity of its older brother, *paint the pickle.* The reason it has never gained much popularity is due to the difficulty of equating paddling with masturbation. Although it shares the threads of power and violence with many other euphemisms for male masturbation, its lack of logic and humor have held it back from becoming more common.

paint the pick·le, v.

1. To apply a liquid mixture, usually of a solid pigment in a liquid vehicle, used as a decorative or protective coating to an edible product, such as a cucumber, that has been preserved and flavored in a solution of brine or vinegar.
2. To coat or decorate a cucumber that had been preserved in brine and various salts with paint.
3. Male masturbation. (slang)

From Middle English *painten,* to paint, from Old French *peintier,* from *peint,* past participle of *peindre,* from Latin *pingere;* Middle English, from Old English *the,* alteration (influenced by *th-,* oblique case stem of demonstrative pronoun), of *se,* masculine demonstrative pronoun. See *so-* in Indo-European roots. See *peig-* in Indo-European roots; and Middle English *pikle,* highly seasoned sauce, probably from Middle Dutch *pekel,* pickle, brine.

EX. George noticed a small blemish in the pickle he was trying to sell to his friend Grant, so he decided to *paint the pickle* to disguise the mark.

Paint the pickle is one of few euphemisms for male masturbation that implies no sense of virility or power. It is merely a representation of the rhythmic motion of masturbation, which is similar to the rhythmic back and forth motion often used in painting. Additionally, the standard reference to the penis as a pickle is present here, serving to reinforce the practicality of this euphemism. Its origin is unknown.

pearl neck·lace, n.

1. An ornament worn around the neck chiefly made up of smooth, lustrous, variously colored deposits, chiefly calcium carbonate, formed around a grain of sand or other foreign matter in the shells of certain mollusks.
2. A sexual act whereby a controlled ejaculation of semen around the neck and shoulders of the recipient leaves small, collected, pools of semen that roughly resemble pearls connected by thins strands of semen left in the dragging of the penis along the skin. (slang)

Middle English *perle,* from Old French, from Latin *pernula,* diminutive of *perna,* ham, seashell (from the shape of the shell); and Middle English *nekke,* from Old English *hnecca,* from Middle English c.1590, from neck (q.v.) + lace in the sense of cord, string.

EX. Johnny gave Becky a *pearl necklace* for their one-year anniversary.

The origins of *pearl necklace,* unlike the majority of other euphemisms, are purely visual. As stated in the definition of pearl necklace, each word in the euphemism refers to the visual results of the sexual act. This euphemism is an anomaly in that sense, since rather than being used as a defense mechanism or an insult, it is purely a visual record, with very few connotations (aside from the very slight implications of the preciousness of semen). Ironically, the term *pearl necklace* is verbally presented as a gift (I will give her a pearl necklace), most likely used by men to foster an insatiable desire for the penis.

Pearl necklace, n.

pick·le smug·gler, n.

1. One who imports or exports an edible product, such as a cucumber, that has been preserved and flavored in a solution of brine or vinegar without paying lawful customs charges or duties.
2. One whose business involves bringing or taking out a solution of brine or vinegar, often spiced, for preserving and flavoring food illicitly or by stealth.
3. Homosexual. (slang)(specifically male)(often considered offensive)

Middle English *pikle*, highly seasoned sauce, probably from Middle Dutch *pekel*, pickle, brine; probably Low German *smukkeln, smuggeln,* or Middle Dutch *smokkelen.*

EX. Ralph wanted to get some pickles across the border, so he hired a *pickle smuggler.*

Pickle smuggler is a direct reference to anal intercourse. Oftentimes smugglers will insert whatever material they are smuggling into the anus for maximum concealment. Given the approximate size and shape of a pickle and its similarity to the penis, it is used here as a term to describe gay men by the act of anal intercourse. This term gained popularity in Texas where border crossings are only loosely patrolled and the primary means of importing illicit materials is for them to be stored in a condom and inserted into the anus (often at customs or in case of accidental arrest).

Pickle smuggler, n.

pil·low bit·er, n.

1. One who cuts, grips, or tears a cloth case, stuffed with something soft, such as down, feathers, or foam rubber, used to cushion the head, with or as if with the teeth.

2. Any person or persons involved in the gripping, cutting into, or injuring of a decorative cushion with or as if with the teeth.

3. Homosexual. (slang)(specifically male)(often considered offensive)

4. Any person engaging in sexual congress. (slang)

Middle English, from Old English *pyle,* from West Germanic *pulw,* from Latin *pulvnus;* Middle English *pille,* from Middle Dutch or Middle Low German *pille,* and Old French *pile,* all from Latin *pilula,* diminutive of *pila,* ball, and Middle English *biten,* from Old English *btan.* See *bheid-* in Indo-European roots.

EX. Maureen worked at the Sears-Roebuck Co. and often saw *pillow biters* coming into the store to taste the pillows.

Pillow biter is an extremely pejorative euphemism used to demean and humiliate homosexual men. It is a direct reference by the heterosexual male to the assumed pain involved with being the recipient of anal intercourse, thereby invalidating the act and deeming it unnatural. Although pillow biter primarily refers to homosexual men, ironically it could easily be used to any recipient of anal sex who finds the process to be painful, pleasurable, or uncomfortable. The term *pillow biter* has been in popular usage since at least the late eighteenth century and refers to the recipient literally biting a pillow during anal intercourse to take their mind off the pain or discomfort (and sometimes to quiet the sounds of pleasure) during the penetration of the anus. It was used as a derogatory remark for homosexual men based on the cultural shame of anal intercourse and the assumption that only gay men partook in it, regardless of the veracity of this belief.

Pills·bur·y dough·boy, n.

1. An immature or inexperienced man, especially a young man made primarily of a soft, thick mixture of dry ingredients, such as flour or meal, and liquid, such as water, that is kneaded, shaped, and baked, especially as bread or pastry, and who is the representative of the C.A. Pillsbury and Co. flour milling company.

2. An advertising icon for C.A. Pillsbury Co. who made his acting debut in 1965. The original voice of the Doughboy was performed by the actor Paul Frees (1920–86). The Doughboy's costar in the commercial was Maureen McCormick.

3. The performance of cunnilingus during an infection of vaginal candidiasis (commonly known as the yeast infection). (slang)

From Charles Alfred Pillsbury (corporate identity); Middle English *dogh,* from Old English *dġ.* See *dheigh-* in Indo-European roots; and Middle English *boi,* possibly from Old French *embuié,* servant, past participle of *embuier,* to fetter.

EX. Shelly loved the *Pillsbury doughboy* ever since she saw it on a crescent roll package when she was a child.

The *Pillsbury doughboy* is a simple, yet graphic reference to the appearance of *Candida Albicans* and *Candida Galbrata* during vaginal candidiasis (commonly known as the vaginal yeast infection). When Pillsbury introduced the creation of Leo Burnett in a Pillsbury crescent rolls commercial in 1965, the 14-ounce, 8 ¾-inch character quickly stole the hearts of American consumers. The cuteness and "pokability" made it a classic candidate for one of the more unsettling sexual practices. The relationship of the cleverness of the euphemism and the perceived crudeness of the sexual act it disguises is generally an inverse one (i.e. the less socially acceptable the behavior, the more clever, and often cute, the euphemism). So, the inherent cuteness of the character and his edible yet still inedible nature lent itself perfectly to the description of performing cunnilingus while the receiving female is presenting vaginal candidiasis.

play·ing the skin flute, v.

1. To perform on a high-pitched woodwind instrument—consisting of a slender tube closed at one end with keys and finger holes on the side and an opening near the closed end across which the breath is blown—that is manufactured with the membranous tissue forming the external covering or integument of an animal and consisting in vertebrates of the epidermis and dermis.

2. To occupy oneself in amusement with any of various similar reedless woodwind instruments, such as the recorder, that are made of or covered by an animal pelt, especially the comparatively pliable pelt of a small or young animal.

3. Fellatio. (slang)

Middle English *playen,* from Old English *plegian.* See *dlegh-* in Indo-European roots; Middle English, from Old Norse *skinn.* See *sek-* in Indo-European roots; and Middle English *floute,* from Old French *flaute,* from Old Provençal *flaüt,* perhaps a blend of *flaujol, flageolet* (from Vulgar Latin *flbeolum,* see *flageolet*), and *laut,* lute, see *lute 1.*

EX. Michelle was a musician and she was an expert in *playing the skin flute.*

Playing the skin flute is one of the many euphemisms that glorify fellatio. Historically, the flute has held a high rank in the cannon of musical instruments since its invention circa 900 B.C.E. The flute became the chosen instrument of the aristocracy in England and France in the early seventeenth century, and was often seen as a mark of one's status (as flutes were finely tooled rather expensive). This cultural desire for flutes was translated into a euphemism due to the similar shape of the flute and the penis and the glorification of and assumed desire of performing fellatio.

pop that (her) cher·ry, v.

1. To burst open a pale yellow to deep red or blackish smooth-skinned drupes enclosing a smooth seed and that belong to any of several varieties, including some cultivated for their fruits or ornamental flowers.
2. To burst open the fruit of the cherry tree, a drupe of various colors and flavors.
3. To take the virginity of a female. (slang)

An amalgamation of Middle English *poppen,* from *pop,* a blow, stroke, of imitative origin; and the Middle English *cheri,* from Anglo-Norman *cherise,* variant of Old French *cerise,* from Vulgar Latin *ceresia,* from *cerasia,* from Greek *kerasi,* cherry tree, from *kerasos.*

EX. Dale was angry with the bartender at work, so he decided to *pop her cherry* so she could not make a Shirley Temple.

Pop that (her) cherry originated from the blood frequently expelled from the vagina after a woman's first experience with intercourse. The blood is from the hymen, a membranous fold of tissue filled with blood that partially or completely occludes the external vaginal orifice, that bursts (pops) during the initial stages of her first intercourse. *Pop that cherry* has implications of shame or lack of chastity due to the ancient tradition of displaying the sheets from the wedding night to prove the purity of a new bride. To protect themselves from violence and even death, some engaged women from cultures with this tradition arrange for hymnography, which is surgery to repair the hymen.

Pop that (her) cherry, v.

post·man (the), n.

1. A man who carries and delivers mail, generally in the employ of the United States Postal Service.
2. One of the two most experienced barristers in the Court of Exchequer, who have precedence in motions, so called from the place where he sits. The other of the two is called the tubman. (legal)
3. Coitus outdoors in any inclement weather (rain, snow, sleet, or hail). (slang)

From Middle English post on notion of riders and horses posted at intervals along a route to speed mail in relays, from Modern French *poste* in this sense (1477). The verb meaning "to send through the postal system" is recorded from 1837. Postmark (noun) is first recorded 1678; postman first recorded 1529.

EX. There was a blizzard in Denver, but *the postman,* James, was still doing his job.

The origins of the *postman* have been attributed to the longtime slogan of the USPS, "Neither rain, nor snow, nor sleet, nor hail, nor dark of night will keep the faithful Postman from the swift completion of his appointed rounds." It has been ironically twisted into a reference surrounding sexual intercourse in any inclement weather. It carries with it a certain sense of masculine pride and virility in the ability to perform at any given time and in any given location. This euphemism is the epitome of homosocial behavior patterns whereby men exhibit their virility for the sake of other men, as in most standard locker-room banter.

punch·ing the munch·kin, v.

1. To hit a very small person with a quick, sharp blow of the fist.
2. To poke or prod an abnormally small person, often having limbs and features atypically proportioned or formed, with or as with a stick.
3. Masturbation. (specifically male) (slang)

Middle English *punchen,* to thrust, prod, prick, from Old French *poinçonner, ponchonner,* to emboss with a punch, from *poinçon, ponchon,* pointed tool. See puncheon; after the Munchkins, characters in *The Wonderful Wizard of Oz* by L. Frank Baum.

EX. When Grant worked as a prop hand for the *Wizard of Oz,* he spent his entire day *punching the munchkin.*

Arguably one of the more amusing euphemisms of our time, *punching the munchkin* arose shortly after the term *munchkin* entered the American vocabulary following the immense popularity of Victor Fleming's 1939 film *The Wizard of Oz.* Punching the munchkin is another of the aggressive and violent euphemisms used to describe male masturbation. A term based on the residents of Munchkin Country in *The Wizard of Oz,* it has since been used to describe dwarfs, children, or anyone of diminutive stature. Using this term to describe the penis is not unlike others that personify the penis as a miniature version of the individual it is attached to. It is not uncommon for any reference to the penis to personify the penis, give it its own identity, and set it aside as an independent entity. The common reason for a euphemism that personifies, autonomizes, and abuses the penis is the male's desire to gain control and dominance over his sexuality, which he feels is an entity apart from himself. This psychological separation of being and sexuality finds expression in a majority of the euphemisms for male masturbation, thereby indicating a mounting problem with the male sexual identity and the conflict inherent within.

Rea·gan·om·ics (the), n.

1. A portmanteau of Reagan and economics; the economic policy put forth and supported by President Ronald Reagan (fortieth president of the United States, 1981–89) based on Reagan's belief in a free-market economy and decreased government spending and regulation.

2. The sudden discharge of semen from the cervix after unprotected intercourse. (slang)

From surname, from Irish *riagan,* literally little king. *Reaganism* first recorded 1966, in reference to policies of Ronald W. *Reagan,* U.S. governor of California, 1967–75, U.S. president, 1981–89; and Middle English *yconomye,* management of a household, from Latin *oeconomia,* from Greek *oikonomi,* from *oikonomos,* manager of a household: *oikos,* house. See *weik-1* in Indo-European roots + *nemein,* to allot, manage. See *nem-in* Indo-European roots.

EX. After Reagan took office, Lauren began to invest all of the money she had saved into stocks. A proponent of *Reaganomics,* Lauren was disappointed to find that her life savings had quickly vanished on Black Monday.

Reaganomics initially began as a both a derisive and supportive term for President Reagan's economic policy of the 1980s. Reaganomics was primarily based on the principles of trickle-down economics. The current usage of Reaganomics has shifted from the realm of economic policy and into the lexicon of sexual euphemisms. The beginning of the usage of Reaganomics as a sexual euphemism occurred toward the end of Reagan's second term in office. The first recorded usage, and subsequent popularity of the term, occurred shortly after Black Monday (October 19, 1987) when the Dow Jones Industrial Average (DJIA) fell over 22 percent, setting a near record single-day drop. The ideas of trickle-down economics and a sudden unsettling drop were deemed appropriate to describe the sudden and often surprising postcoital expulsion of semen from the cervix. The "trickle-down" (which only occurs after unprotected intercourse) also carries with it implications of Black Monday only occurring in an unprotected economy. Once introduced into the American vernacular, the Reaganomics, much like the stock market crash of Black Monday, quickly spread to Canada, Australia, and the United Kingdom.

rid·ing the Her·shey high·way, v.

1. To travel over a main public road, especially one connecting towns and cities made of or paved with the chocolate confection created by Milton Snavely Hershey.
2. To be carried or conveyed, as in a vehicle or on horseback over a major road in Hershey, Pennsylvania.
3. Anal intercourse. (slang)

Middle English *riden,* from Old English *rdan.* See *reidh-* in Indo-European roots; and Old English *heiweg,* main road from one town to another, and *hearch,* Middle English from Old English *hrshai*, from vulgar Latin *hshrn.* See *chcn* fron Indo-European roots.

EX. On the way back to Ohio from New York, Jack and Kelly were *riding the Hershey highway.*

Riding the Hershey highway refers to the darker color of the skin surrounding the anus and the area between the buttocks. Not surprisingly, this euphemism originated in Pennsylvania near Lancaster as the working class grew increasingly bitter over layoffs by the area's primary employer, the Hershey chocolate maker which had decided to automate many of its production processes. The term was an attempt to regain dignity by equating the owner of the company, Milton Snavely Hershey, with feces and homosexuality.

ro·de·o, n.

1. A public competition or exhibition in which skills such as riding broncos or roping calves are displayed.

2. A public performance featuring bronco riding, calf roping, steer wrestling, and Brahma bull riding.

3. Attempting to maintain penetration of the recipient for eight seconds after informing him or her of your sexual encounters with any relative or close friend of the recipient.

Spanish, *corral, rodeo,* from *rodear,* to surround, from *rueda,* wheel, from Latin *rota.* See *ret-* in Indo-European roots.

EX. Crazy Jake Thomas was the best *rodeo* rider in all of West Texas.

The *rodeo,* also known as the eight seconds, is a euphemism that is steeped in the rich cultural history of the old American West. The first organized rodeo was recorded in Deer Trail, Colorado, in 1864 and was a display or competition of skills used in the daily life of cowboys. Although it may seem like an arbitrary time, the rodeo standard of eight seconds as the qualification for a successful ride is devised for the safety of the animal, not as commonly believed for the safety of the rider. After eight seconds the bull has used up the majority of its adrelanine and risks suffering from fatigue, or being tamed. Ironically this carries over into the use of the rodeo as a sexual practice. When the male (penetrating the recipient from behind) informs the recipient that his or her wife, sister, father, mother, brother, child (or any other person close to the recipient) performs better sexually than the recipient, the objective of remaining inside the recipient for eight seconds becomes the primary goal. In this situation ejaculation is a bonus, but not a required event for the successful completion of the rodeo. The importance of official rodeo time has retained the same objective of not exhausting, hurting, or taming the recipient.

rug munch·er (also car·pet munch·er), n.

1. One who chews heavy fabric used to cover a floor, audibly or with a steady working of the jaws.
2. One who masticates and consumes a thick heavy covering for a floor, usually made of woven wool or synthetic fibers.
3. One who performs cunnilingus. (slang)
4. Lesbian. (slang)

Middle English, from Old French *carpite,* from Medieval Latin *carpta,* from Old Italian *rog,* from *rge,* to pluck, from Latin *regger,* from Old Italian *carpita,* from *carpire,* to pluck, from Latin *carpere.* See *kerp-* in Indo-European roots. See *rg-* in Indo-European roots, and Middle English *monchen.*

EX. Big Bob was hungry while he was at work, so he called up a friend who was a *rug muncher* to get a tip on the best flavor of the Anso crush stain-resistor carpet.

Rug muncher began its evolution as slang for homosexual females. Since the euphemism itself gave no indication of the gender of the active participant, it quickly became a more widely used euphemism to discuss any and all cunnilingus. The pubis mons, due to location, texture, and quantity of pubic hair, has been referred to as the "rug" or "carpet" since the invention of modern carpeting. Given the use of rug and the actions involved with cunnilingus (moving jaw, tongue, and teeth), it quickly came a popular term.

Rug munch·er (also carpet munch·er), n.

rump rang·er, n.

1. A member of an armed troop employed in patroling the fleshy hindquarters of an animal.
2. A member of a group of U.S. soldiers specially trained for making raids of the upper rounded part of the hindquarters of a quadruped mammal either on foot, in ground vehicles, or by airlift.
3. Homosexual. (slang) (specifically male) (often considered offensive)
4. Any purveyor of anal intercourse. (slang)

Middle English *rumpe,* of Scandinavian origin, and 1388, "gameskeeper," from range. Attested to from 1670 in sense of "man (often mounted) who polices an area." Modern military sense of "member of an elite U.S. combat unit" originated in 1942 (organized 1941).

EX. Last week, after Grandma Jones made her famous rump roast, someone stole it. This week she hired *rump rangers* to protect her valuable treasure.

The origin of *rump ranger* is rooted in the patroling, inspection, and raiding that rangers are known for. It is believed that the standard modus operandi (MO) of the U.S. Army Rangers is to circle an area, make sure the region is safe, and attack. The use of ranger in this slang came from the terminology used by the U.S. Army Rangers when making an attack. After the initial area scans, they make a small "insertion" of two teams of two troops, proceeded by the rest of the team. Rump ranger was born in late 1940s when the use of this terminology by the U.S. Army Rangers became somewhat common knowledge. Rump had been used to describe the posterior for approximately 300 years prior to the addition of ranger.

Rump ranger, n.

rust·y trom·bone, n.

1. A brass instrument consisting of a long cylindrical tube bent upon itself twice, ending in a bell-shaped mouth, and having a movable U-shaped slide for producing different pitches, which has been covered with rust and corroded.

2. A combination of two relatively common sexual acts. While performing analingis, the active party (indicated by the performance of sexual acts) reaches around to the penis and simultaneously stimulates the penis and testicles with the free hand(s). (slang)

Middle English, from Old English *rst*. See *reudh-* in Indo-European roots; and French, from Italian, augmentative of *tromba,* trumpet, of Germanic origin.

EX. Danny's family was poor, so they could only afford to get him a *rusty trombone.*

Surprisingly, the *rusty trombone* is not one of the more contemporary sexual euphemisms. Given its graphic nature, it is easy to assume that the euphemism originated after the sexual revolution of the 1960s and 1970s. However the usage of rusty trombone predates the sexual revolution by almost thirty years. The rusty trombone was at the height of its popularity in Harlem in the late 1930s during the golden age of jazz. Poor musicians often played with substandard instruments and would have to make do with what they had. One industrious musician performing at Minton's Playhouse in Harlem claimed that his rusted trombone was not dissimilar to the hindquarters of a horse. Although this preemptive qualification of his notably wonderful performance passed without notice, the term *rusty trombone* quickly invaded jive talk and became one of the more popular phrases. The simplicity of content and ease of visual reference, helped the rusty trombone gain popularity outside of jive talk and enter into the American vernacular.

shoot·ing put·ty at the moon, v.

1. The act of discharging a doughlike cement, made by mixing whiting and linseed oil, from a weapon or device aimed toward a natural satellite revolving around a planet.
2. To propel forward rapidly a fine lime cement used as a finishing coat on plaster in the direction of the natural satellite of the Earth.
3. Male masturbation. (slang)

Middle English *shoten,* from Old English *scotan.* See *skeud-* in Indo-European roots. Interjection, alteration of shit; French *potée,* polishing powder, from Old French, *a potful, from pot, pot,* from Vulgar Latin *pottus,* and the Middle English *moone,* from Old English *mna.* See m^2 in Indo-European roots.

EX. Ryan was a wasteful carpenter, so instead of saving the remaining putty from his drywall job, he spent an entire evening *shooting putty at the moon.*

Shooting putty at the moon is another in a large collection of euphemisms for male masturbation that are aggressive and powerful. The implication that the ejaculate could reach the moon is an indication of the masculine attachment to power and sexual prowess. The putty is a clear reference in color and texture of semen, and the use of shooting implies ejaculation. Being one of the more clever euphemisms in its implications of male virility and strength it has become almost commonplace.

smok·ing sau·sage, v.

1. To draw in and exhale smoke from a finely chopped and seasoned meat, especially pork, usually stuffed into a prepared animal intestine or other casing, and cooked or cured.
2. To engage in smoking seasoned meat, usually prepared in a casing of intestines, regularly or habitually.
3. Fellatio. (slang)

Middle English, from Old English *smoca;* and Middle English *sausige,* from Anglo-Norman *sausiche,* from Vulgar Latin *salscia,* from Late Latin, neuter plural of *salscius,* prepared by salting, from *salsus,* salted.

EX. In an attempt to preserve the meat that his family had for the winter, Jeremy spent all afternoon *smoking sausage.*

The penis has been referred to as the meat or the sausage for centuries. The particular shape of a sausage (link) and the method in which it is eaten (introduced at an angle perpendicular to the mouth) is easily considered sexual in nature. When tobacco came to Europe from the new colonies and gained popularity, the sophisticated nature of smoking made it ironically ripe for a sexual euphemism. The action of drawing smoke into the mouth by motion of the cheeks was seen as similar to the pressure applied by the active participant of fellatio. Naturally, *smoking sausage* came to mimic the size and shape of the penis and the actions of fellatio to form one of the most common and prevalent euphemisms in modern vernacular.

Smoking sausage, v.

snail trail, n.

1. A marked or beaten path, as through woods or wilderness, primarily used by any of numerous aquatic or terrestrial mollusks of the class Gastropoda.

2. A mark, trace, course, or path left by the moving body of a mollusk typically having a spiral-coiled shell, broad retractile foot, and distinct head.

3. Labia. (slang)

Middle English, from Old English *snægl;* and Middle English *trailen,* probably from Old French *trailler,* to hunt without a foreknown course, from Vulgar Latin *trgulre,* to make a deer double back and forth, perhaps alteration (influenced by Latin *trgula,* dragnet), of Latin *trahere,* to pull, draw.

EX. Charles was studying the habits of modern terrestrial mollusks and he would locate them by following the *snail trails* left in the woods.

Snail trail originated in Britain in the late eighteenth century as waves of biologists and explorers were returning from the African rain forests. They had encountered large mollusks that left a shiny and slimy trail in their wake. Upon their return, the sight of an engorged, lubricated vagina reminded them of the remnants of a traveling snail. The comical nature of the euphemism and its use of unappealing descriptors for the female genitalia made it quickly popular. This euphemism, like many for the vagina, is generally unappealing. The use of these types of euphemisms is to ascribe shame to female sexuality while exalting male power and control (male euphemisms are generally powerful).

sug·ar in the (his) shoes, n.

1. A sweet crystalline or powdered substance, white when pure, consisting of sucrose obtained mainly from sugar cane and sugar beet contained within a durable covering for the human foot, made of leather or similar material with a rigid sole and heel.

2. Any of a class of water-soluble crystalline carbohydrates, including sucrose and lactose, having a characteristically sweet taste contained within a covering for the human foot, usually made of leather, having a thick and somewhat stiff sole and a lighter top.

3. Homosexual male. (slang) (specifically male) (often considered offensive)

Middle English *sugre,* from Old French *sukere,* from Medieval Latin *succrum,* from Old Italian *zucchero,* from Arabic *sukkar,* from Persian *shakar,* from Sanskrit *arkar,* grit, ground sugar; and Middle English, from Old English *sch.*

EX. When Noah got home from the factory every day, he had almost a pound of *sugar in his shoes.*

Sugar in the shoes originates from the longtime use of "sweet" to emasculate men, thereby conferring on them a diminished status among their peers. It is not for men to be sweet and sensitive, so this term evolved to describe a man who was sweet to the point that sugar had settled in the bottom of his shoes, as though he were dripping with homosexuality. It is one of many euphemisms that reinforces traditional masculine stereotypes through the degradation of females or homosexuals.

Sugar in the (his) shoes, n.

sweat·er pup·pies, n.

1. A young dog who resides in a jacket or pullover made especially of knit, crocheted, or woven wool, cotton, or synthetic yarn.
2. A young domestic dog, specifically less than one year old, who is present in a crocheted or knitted garment covering the upper part of the body.
3. Breasts. (slang)

From Old English *sweati* and Vulgar Latin *switi* (to sweat), "woolen vest or jersey, originally worn in rowing," 1882, from earlier *sweaters,* "clothing worn to produce sweating and reduce weight," 1828, from *sweat;* and Middle English *popi,* small pet dog, perhaps from Anglo-Norman *poppe,* doll, from Vulgar Latin *puppa,* from Latin *ppa,* girl, doll.

EX. Rose had a set of *sweater puppies* that all of her friends like to pet.

A simple and almost cute euphemism, *sweater puppies* is one of the many that seek to personify the breasts. This phenomenon is intended to demystify the breasts and recontextualize them as something familiar and easily understandable. Sweater puppies originated in the mid twentieth century when the popularity of sweaters reached its peak, and sweaters became more form fitting. The choice to analogize breasts to puppies is a reference to the appeal of both objects and a visual analogy to the size of (at the time ideal) C-cup breasts and the comparable size of a young puppy snuggled into the shirt.

tak·ing the skin boat to tu·na town, v.

1. To carry, convey, lead, or cause to go along to another place in a relatively small, usually open craft of a size that might be carried aboard a ship often called an umiak, which is made of stretched animal pelt, especially the comparatively pliable pelt of a small or young animal, to a population center that is larger than a village and smaller than a city, known for any of various often large scombroid marine food and game fishes of the genus *Thunnus* and related genera, many of which, including *T. thynnus* and the albacore, are commercially important sources of canned fish.

2. To transport any inland vessel made of stretched skin to an area that is more densely populated or developed than the surrounding area, which produces edible flesh of tuna, often canned or processed.

3. Coitus. (slang)

Middle English *taken,* from Old English *tacan,* from Old Norse *taka,* Middle English, from Old Norse *skinn.* See *sek-* in Indo-European roots; Middle English *bot,* from Old English *bt.* See *bheid-* in Indo-European roots; American Spanish, from Spanish *atún,* from Arabic *at-tn,* the tuna, from Latin *thunnus,* and Middle English, from Old English *tn,* enclosed place, village. See *dheu-* in Indo-European roots.

EX. Ivanho was a Viking sailor who would spend his days *taking the skin boat to tuna town* to keep his family fed.

One of the simplest, and most slanted, euphemisms is *taking the skin boat to tuna town.* This euphemism, like many others, glorifies the need for the penis while casting the vagina as dirty and/or unsanitary. The comparison of the penis to a skin boat is twofold. The skin boat (examples include the umiak, klepper, biadarka, curragh, and coracle) was the first type of sailing vessel (which consisted of skin stretched over a hard frame) and was a prized possession of any person or family. It allowed the owners to fish with greater ease, explore islands and inlets, and generally improved the quality of life.

These implications are carried forward into this historical euphemism, the penis is described by its value and appearance. Contrarily, the female sexual organs are described by their odor, which is commonly described as "fishy" or like tuna.

tea bag, v.

1. To make a slightly bitter beverage by steeping tea leaves in boiling water, which have been put into or as if into a bag.
2. To place into a bag any of various beverages, made by steeping the leaves of certain plants or by extracting an infusion especially from leaves.
3. To draw testicles into the mouth by movements of the tongue and lips that create suction. (slang)

Probably from the Dutch *thee,* from Malay *teh,* from Chinese (Amoy) *te* (equivalent to Mandarin Chinese *chá*); and Middle English *bagge,* from Old Norse *baggi.*

EX. Amy could not talk to Johnny when he came over because she was busy *tea bagging* her favorite Earl Grey.

The slang *tea bag* most likely originated from the English practice of placing the remainder of a bag of tea in one's mouth after finishing the liquid to suck out the last few (and generally very potent) drops of the steeped beverage. The use of tea bag as a reference to the testicles is not a new practice and originated in the early twentieth century due to their similar shape when wet (as the wet tea bag has a somewhat drooped shape due to the settling of the leaves).

tick·le the beard·ed clam, v.

1. To touch the soft edible body of a mollusk that possesses a hairy or hairlike growth, such as that appearing on or near the face of certain animals, lightly, so as to cause laughter or twitching movements.

2. To tease or excite pleasurably any number of burrowing marine and freshwater mollusks of the class Pelecypoda that are furnished with facial hair.

3. To tease or pleasurably stimulate the clitoris. (slang) (female masturbation)

Middle English *tikelen,* perhaps frequentative of *ticken,* to touch lightly, Middle English *berd,* from Old English *beard.* See *bhardh-* in Indo-European roots; and Middle English, from Old English *clam, clamm,* bond, fetter.

EX. "Jenny, do not *tickle the bearded clam* at the dinner table!" her mother exclaimed.

Tickle the bearded clam originates from the old French reference to clam for the female sexual organs. The term was used by the French peasantry in the late eighteenth century as a descriptor of the approximate size, shape, and smell of the labia (which was seen to be similar to an uncooked clam). The term gained popularity in the British Isles in the early nineteenth century and quickly spread with the addition of tickle, which was almost a forgone conclusion due to the similar motions of repeated flicking and/or rubbing in the stimulation of a sensitive area.

Tickle the bearded clam, v.

toss·ing sal·ad, v.

1. To throw lightly or casually or with a sudden slight jerk a dish of raw leafy green vegetables, often tossed with pieces of other raw or cooked vegetables, fruit, cheese, or other ingredients and served with a dressing.
2. To throw, fling, or heave continuously about a cold dish of chopped vegetables, fruit, meat, fish, eggs, or other food, usually prepared with a dressing, such as mayonnaise.
3. Analingus. (slang)

From Middle English *tossen,* possibly of Scandinavian origin; and Middle English *salade,* from Old French, possibly from Old Provençal *salada,* from Vulgar Latin *salta,* from feminine past participle of *salre,* to salt, from Latin *sl,* salt. See *sal-* in Indo-European roots.

EX. Carolyn came home to find her husband, Mike, *tossing salad* for their dinner.

A derivation of eating out, *tossing salad* is a derogatory term aimed at emasculating homosexual men, by implying that because of their sexual orientation, they are inherently less masculine. When this euphemism was popularized, it only described the act of a man performing analingus on another man. The propagation of the term stemmed from the results of mixing various greens and dressing to achieve an even coating on each leaf. It was assumed that this type of care and precision was taken to coat the anus in saliva and prepare the anus for anal intercourse. It is this logical leap that hindered the initial popularity of tossing salad and why its origin still remains a mystery to so many. Tossing salad soon came to describe any sessions of analingus where the tongue penetrates the sphincter (thereby differentiating it from a "rim job") regardless of intentions of anal intercourse.

Tro·jan Horse, n.

1. The hollow wooden horse in which, according to legend, Greeks hid to gain entrance to Troy, later opening the gates to their army.

2. A program that appears to be legitimate but is designed to have destructive effects to the data residing in the computer onto which the program was loaded.

3. An act whereby the male perforates the tip of a condom to induce insemination of the female he is engaging in sexual relations with. (slang)

Middle English, from Latin *Trinus,* from Tria *Troy,* from Greek, from *Trs,* the mythical founder of Troy; Middle English, from Old English *hors.*

EX. General Simmons was planning to attack Canada, and planned his operation based on the mythical story of the *Trojan Horse.*

The *Trojan Horse* is a euphemism entirely reflective of its moniker. The subtleties of the euphemism lie in the finer points of history regarding the legend of the Trojan Horse. The origins of the euphemism date back to the early seventeenth century almost immediately following the invention of the condom. There was an obsession with Greek and Roman culture that bred interest in their mythology. Men would try to father children in order to carry on the family name, and they would do this by sabotaging the prophylactics. The Trojan Horse relies on a cursory understanding of history, wherein the soldiers (semen) snuck in and attacked (impregnated) the city of Troy when the horse was brought in as a peace offering. The assumption and understanding of the penis as a gift or treat is a common practice in euphemisms to enhance the perceived preciousness of the male genitalia.

turd bur·glar, n.

1. One who commits burglary of excrement.
2. One who enters a building or premises with the intent to commit the theft of feces.
3. Homosexual. (slang) (specifically male) (often considered offensive)
4. Any patron of anal intercourse. (slang) (not specifically homosexual)

Combination of origins of the Anglo-French *burglarie,* modification of Medieval Latin *burgaria,* from *burgare,* to break into (a house); and the Middle English, from Old English *tord.* See *der-* in Indo-European roots. Recontextualized as American slang in the early twentieth century.

EX. Betsy observed the man in the alley and thought, "That must be the saddest *turd burglar* in the whole world."

The use of *turd burglar* as slang is rooted in the interaction with feces during anal intercourse. Given the climate of the Protestant Reformation when this term came into popularity, the addition of burglar (which had strong implications of a lack of morality) was an effective addition, although not wholly accurate since those who engage in sexual congress (anal) do not specifically seek possession of their partner's feces.

Turd burglar, n.

wax that ass, v.

1. To make smooth and shiny the hoofed mammals of the genus *Equus,* resembling and closely related to horses but having a smaller build and longer ears, and including the domesticated donkey, by rubbing.
2. To remove unwanted hair from an animal resembling a small horse with long ears, sometimes used as a beast of burden by using heated wax that is left to dry and then removed.
3. Coitus. (slang)

From Middle English *waxen,* from Old English *weaxan.* See *aug-* in Indo-European roots; and Middle English *ars,* from Old English *ears.* See *ors-* in Indo-European roots.

EX. Nicole wanted her pet donkey to shine at the county fair, so she decided to *wax that ass* before she left for the fairgrounds.

There are two viable theories of the origin of *wax that ass.* The more literal, and first origin, uses the word wax in another context. Traditionally, it was used to describe the gradual increase in intensity or size of something (i.e. the moon). The previous existence of "mooning" described as gradually showing someone your posterior is the formal root of wax that ass. The sexual connotation of someone gradually removing their clothes letting their ass wax leaves expectations of pending sexual congress, hence the first origin. The second, and more modern, is rooted in American slang. Wax is used in the context of the motions used in waxing (generally an automobile) and the similar actions in the spanking of the recipient when two are engaged in the sexual position known as "doggie style."

Wax that ass, v.

yo·del·ing in the val·ley, v.

1. To sing so that the voice fluctuates rapidly between the normal chest voice and a falsetto while sitting or standing in an elongated lowland between ranges of mountains, hills, or other uplands, often having a river or stream running along the bottom.
2. To sing (a song) by yodeling, taking advantage of the natural acoustics of an extensive area of land drained or irrigated by a river system.
3. Cunnilingus. (slang)

German *jodeln,* from German dialectal *jo,* exclamation of delight, of imitative origin; and Middle English *valey,* from Old French *valee,* from Vulgar Latin *vallta,* from Latin *valls.* See *wel* in Indo-European roots.

EX. Stephanie was inspired by a commercial she saw on television and decided to go out to the country and spend the day *yodeling in the valley* with some friends.

Yodeling in the valley originated from the Swiss practice of taking advantage of the natural acoustics of eroded land to carry the high and oscillating pitches of traditional yodeling. It stemmed from a mockery of promiscuous women (often called loose) and the belief that women who had engaged in intercourse with multiple partners possessed larger (implied as gaping) vaginas. The use of valley also is a descriptor of the shape of a vagina and its ability to naturally lubricate (referencing the formation of valleys). Yodeling was adopted because the repetitive opening and closing of the mouth while performing cunnilingus closely resembles the labial motions involved with yodeling (the guttural aspect of yodeling is ignored in this euphemism).

GLOSSARY

anal: Of, relating to, or near the anus.

anus: The opening at the lower end of the alimentary canal through which solid waste is eliminated from the body.

bisexual: Of, relating to, or having a sexual orientation to persons of either sex.

coitus: Sexual union between a male and a female involving insertion of the penis into the vagina.

clitoris: A small, elongated erectile organ at the anterior part of the vulva, homologous with the penis.

congress: Sexual intercourse.

cunnilingus: Oral stimulation of the clitoris or vulva.

erect: Being in a vertical, upright position.

erection: The firm and enlarged condition of a body organ or part when the erectile tissue surrounding it becomes filled with blood, especially such a condition of the penis or clitoris.

feces: Waste matter eliminated from the bowels; excrement.

fellatio: Oral stimulation of the penis.

homosexual: Of, relating to, or having a sexual orientation to persons of the same sex.

irrumatio: Oral stimulation of the penis whereby the mouth acts as a passive receptacle for the thrusting penis.

intercourse: Sexual intercourse.

labia: The four folds of tissue of the female external genitalia.

lesbian: A woman whose sexual orientation is to women.

masturbation: Excitation of one's own or another's genital organs, usually to orgasm, by manual contact or means other than sexual intercourse.

penis: The male organ of copulation in higher vertebrates, homologous with the clitoris. In mammals, it also serves as the male organ of urinary excretion.

semen: A viscous whitish secretion of the male reproductive organs, containing spermatozoa and consisting of secretions of the testes, seminal vesicles, prostate, and bulbourethral glands.

sexual: Of, relating to, involving, or characteristic of sex, sexuality, the sexes, or the sex organs and their functions.

spermatozoa: The mature fertilizing gamete of a male organism, usually consisting of a round or cylindrical nucleated cell, a short neck, and a thin motile tail.

vagina: The passage leading from the opening of the vulva to the cervix of the uterus in female mammals.